Art of Retailing

Published by
Lotus Press Publishers & Distributors

Art of Retailing

Arun Mahapatra

Lotus Press
4735/22, Prakash Deep Building,
Ansari Road, Daryaganj,
New Delhi - 110002

Lotus Press Publishers & Distributors
Unit No.220, 2nd Floor, 4735/22, Prakash Deep Building,
Ansari Road, Daryaganj, New Delhi- 110002
Ph:- 32903912, 23280047, 098118-38000
Email : lotuspress1984@gmail.com
Visit us : www.lotuspress.co.in

Art of Retailing

ISBN : 978-81-8382-208-4

Published by : **Lotus Press Publishers & Distributors,** New Delhi- 2
Printed at : **Bharat Offset Works,** New Delhi

PREFACE

Retailing consists of the sale of goods or merchandise from a fixed location, such as a department store or kiosk, or by post, in small or individual lots for direct consumption by the purchaser. Retailing may include subordinated services, such as delivery. Purchasers may be individuals or businesses. In commerce, a retailer buys goods or products in large quantities from manufacturers or importers, either directly or through a wholesaler, and then sells smaller quantities to the end-user. Retail establishments are often called shops or stores. Retailers are at the end of the supply chain. Manufacturing marketers see the process of retailing as a necessary part of their overall distribution strategy.

Considering the various sociocultural and economic forces that inform enterprises today, such as globalisation and competition, retailing has come about to acquire the status of almost art. The book thereby is intended not just as an incisive referral which looks into the various processes which go into the enterprise of retailing, but as a manual which seeks to guide readers through the art and science of retailing in an intensely competitive environment. Supplemented with various case-studies and examples, the book goes into extensive analysis of the various facets of retailing, and undertakes comprehending the various challenges and rules which underpin the field. It is hoped that the incisive content of the book is appreciated by all.

Editor

CONTENTS

1

INTRODUCTION TO RETAILING

Retailing consists of the sale of goods or merchandise from a fixed location, such as a departmental store or kiosk, or by post, in small or individual lots for direct consumption by the purchaser. Retailing may include subordinated services, such as delivery. Purchasers may be individuals or businesses. In commerce, a retailer buys goods or products in large quantities from manufacturers or importers, either directly or through a wholesaler, and then sells smaller quantities to the end-user. Retail establishments are often called shops or stores. Retailers are at the end of the supply chain. Manufacturing marketers see the process of retailing as a necessary part of their overall distribution strategy.

Shops may be on residential streets, shopping streets with few or no houses, or in a shopping centre or mall. Shopping streets may be for pedestrians only. Sometimes a shopping street has a partial or full roof to protect customers from precipitation. Online retailing, also referred to as B2C type of e-commerce, and mail order are forms of non-shop retailing.

Shopping generally refers to the act of buying products. Sometimes this is done to obtain necessities such as food and clothing; sometimes it is done as a recreational activity. Recreational shopping often involves window shopping (just looking, not buying) and browsing and does not always result in a purchase.

NATURE OF RETAILING

Retailing is the final link between the production of a good and the end-consumer. The economic characteristics of the end-consumer are thus crucial to the economics of retailing. Typically, the end-consumer can be characterised as being:

1. Small (in the sense that the size of a given purchase forms a small part both of the consumer's total expenditure and of the retailer's total sales);
2. Immobile (in the sense that they are often not able or willing to travel long distances in order to purchase the appropriate product); and
3. Uninformed (in the sense that they often do not know which products are available where, and on what prices; and they may not be able to observe product quality in advance of purchase). The combination of these characteristics explains essentially why retailers exist.

   The fact that consumers' purchases tend to be small means that retailers play an important role in preventing the exploitation of consumers by manufacturers: no single consumer would have any bargaining power against powerful manufacturers, whereas retailers can bargain strongly on their behalf.

   The fact that consumers are immobile means that retailers play an important function in bringing the products to the consumers, to prevent the consumer from having to go to the product. The fact that consumers are uninformed about the availability of products, their prices, and their qualities means that retailers carry out an important service in terms of providing information and quality assurances.

These characteristics also explain many aspects of retailing. For example, consumers' immobility means that geographical location and one-stop shopping will be important, while their lack of information means that price visibility, product range, and reputation/quality assurances will be important.

These aspects of retailing feed straight into a discussion of the nature of competition in retailing. There are four dimensions of horizontal competition between retailers:

1. Pricing;
2. Geographical location;
3. Product selection; and
4. Retailer service.

These various dimensions in retailing have important consequences for competition policy, and it is crucial, when considering competition in retailing, to examine all of these dimensions.

RETAIL PRICING

The pricing technique used by most retailers is cost-plus pricing. This involves adding a markup amount (or percentage) to the retailers cost. Another common technique is suggested retail pricing. This simply involves charging the amount suggested by the manufacturer and usually printed on the product by the manufacturer.

In Western countries, retail prices are often called psychological prices or odd prices. Often prices are fixed and displayed on signs or labels. Alternatively, there can be price discrimination for a variety of reasons, where the retailer charges higher prices to some customers and lower prices to others. For example, a customer may have to pay more if the seller determines that he or she is willing to. The retailer may conclude this due to the customer's wealth, carelessness, lack of knowledge, or eagerness to buy. Another example is the practice of discounting for youths or students.

Transfer Mechanism

There are several ways in which consumers can receive goods from a retailer:

— Counter service, where goods are out of reach of buyers, and must be obtained from the seller. This type of retail is common for small expensive items (e.g. jewellery) and controlled items like medicine and liquor. It was common before the 1900s in the United States, and is more common in certain countries.

— Delivery (commerce), where goods are shipped directly to consumer's homes or workplaces. Mail order from a printed catalogue was invented in 1744 and common in the late 1800s and early 1900s. Ordering by telephone is now common, either from a catalogue, newspaper or television advertisement, or local restaurant menu for immediate service. Direct marketing and television shopping channels are also used to generate telephone orders. Online shopping started gaining significant market share in developed countries in the 2000s.

— Door-to-door sales, where the salesperson sometimes travels with the goods for sale.

— Self-service, where goods may be handled and examined prior to purchase, has become more common since the 1920s.

Building Types

A market is a physical location where buyers and sellers converge. Usually this is done in town squares, sidewalks or designated streets and may involve the construction of temporary structures (market stalls). Markets are contrasted with shop or store trading, where a retailer has a permanent, dedicated building. Buildings for retail have changed considerably over time. Market halls were constructed in the Middle Ages, which were essentially just covered marketplaces. The first shops in the modern sense used to deal with just one type of article, and usually adjoined the producer (baker, tailor, cobbler). In the U.S., retailers often provided boardwalks in front of their stores to protect customers from the mud. In the 19th century, in France, arcades were invented, which were a street of several different shops, roofed over. Counters, each dealing with a different kind of article, were invented; it was called a departmental store. One of the novelties of the departmental store was the introduction of fixed prices, making haggling unnecessary, and browsing more enjoyable. This is commonly considered the birth of consumerism. In cities, these were multi-story buildings which pioneered the escalator.

In the 1920s the first supermarket opened in the United States, heralding in a new era of retail: self-service. Around the same time the first shopping mall was constructed which incorporated elements from both the arcade and the departmental store. A mall consists of several departmental stores linked by arcades. The design was perfected by the Austrian architect Victor Gruen. All the stores rent their space from the mall owner. By mid-century, most of these were being developed as single enclosed, climate-controlled, projects in suburban areas. The mall has had a considerable impact on the retail structure and urban development in Western countries.

Physical shops are known as brick and mortar stores in America, when contrasting them with online stores. Many shops are part of a chain: a number of similar shops with the same name selling the same products in different locations. The shops may be owned by one company, or there may be a franchising company that has franchising agreements with the shop owners.

GENRES OF RETAIL

Some shops sell second-hand goods. In other cases, especially in the case of a nonprofit shop, the public donates goods to the shop to be sold. In give-away shops goods can be taken for free. There are also "consignment" shops, which are where a person can place an item in a store, and if it sells the person gives the shop owner a percentage of the sale price. The advantage of selling an item this way is that the established shop gives the item exposure to more potential buyers.

The term "retailer" is also applied where a service provider services the needs of a large number of individuals, such as a public utility like electric power.

Sales Techniques

Behind the scenes at retail there is another factor at work. Corporations and independent store owners alike are always trying to get the edge on their competitors. One way to do this is to hire a merchandising solutions company to design custom store displays that will attract more customers in a certain demographic. The nation's largest retailers spend millions every year on in-store marketing programmes that correspond to season and promotional changes. As products change, so will a retail landscape.

Retailers may use facing to create the look of a perfectly-stocked store even when it is not. A destination store is one that customers will initiate a trip specifically to visit, sometimes over a large area. These stores are often used to "anchor" a shopping mall or plaza, generating foot traffic which is capitalised on by smaller retailers.

CONCERNS OF RETAILERS

Retailers are faced with many issues as they attempt to be successful. The key issues include:

— *Customer satisfaction* – Retailers know that satisfied customers are loyal customers. Consequently, retailers must develop strategies intended to build relationships that result in customers returning to make more purchases.

— *Ability to acquire the right products* – A customer will only be satisfied if they can purchase the right products to satisfy their needs. Since a large percentage of retailers do not manufacture their own products, they must seek suppliers who will supply products demanded by customers. Thus, an important objective for retailers is to identify the products customers will demand and negotiate with suppliers to obtain these products.

— *Product presentation* – Once obtained products must be presented or merchandised to customers in a way that generates interest. Retail merchandising often requires hiring creative people who understand and can relate to the market.

— *Traffic building* – Like any marketer, retailers must use promotional methods to build customer interest. For retailers a key measure of interest is the number of people visiting a retail location or website. Building "traffic" is accomplished with a variety of promotional techniques such as advertising, including local newspapers or Internet, and specialised promotional activities, such as coupons.

— *Layout*– For store-based retailers a store's physical layout is an important component in creating a retail experience that will attract customers. The physical layout is more than just deciding in what part of the store to locate products. For many retailers designing the right shopping atmosphere (e.g., objects, light, sound) can add to the appeal of a store. Layout is also important in the online world where site navigation and usability may be deciding factors in whether of a retail website is successful.

— *Location* – Where to physically locate a retail store may help or hinder store traffic. Well placed stores with high visibility and easy access, while possibly commanding higher land usage fees, may hold significantly more value than lower cost sites that yield less traffic. Understanding the trade-off between costs and benefits of locations is an important retail decision.

— *Keeping pace with technology* – Technology has invaded all areas of retailing including customer knowledge (e.g., customer relationship management software), product movement (e.g., use of RFID tags for tracking), point-of-purchase (e.g., scanners, kiosks, self-serve checkout), web technologies (e.g., online shopping carts, purchase recommendations) and many more.

WAYS TO CATEGORISE RETAILERS

There are many ways retailers can be categorised depending on the characteristics being evaluated. There are six factors directly related to major marketing decisions:

- — target markets served
- — product offerings
- — pricing structure
- — promotional emphasis
- — distribution method
- — service level

and one operational factor:

- — ownership

However, these groups are not meant to be mutually exclusive. In fact, as we will see in some way all retailers can placed into each category.

Target Markets Served

The first classification looks at the type of markets a retailer intends to target.

- — *Mass market* – Mass market retailers appeal to the largest market possible by selling products of interest to nearly all consumers. With such a large market from which to draw customers, the competition among these retailers is often fierce.
- — *Speciality market* – Retailers categorised as servicing the speciality market are likely to target buyers looking for products having certain features that go beyond mass marketed products, such as customers who require more advanced product options or higher level of customer service. While not as large as the mass market, the target market serviced by speciality retailers can be sizable.
- — *Exclusive market* – Appealing to this market means appealing to discriminating customers who are often willing to pay a premium for features found in very few products and for highly personalised services. Since this target market is small, the

number of retailers addressing this market within a given geographic area may also be small.

Products Carried

Under this classification retailers are divided based on the width (i.e., number of different product lines) and depth (i.e., number of different products within a product line) of the products they carry.

- *General merchandisers* – These retailers carry a wide range of product categories (i.e., broad width) though the number of different items within a particular product line is generally limited (i.e., shallow depth).
- *Multiple lines speciality merchandisers* — Retailers classified in this category stock a limited number of product lines (i.e., narrow width) but within the categories they handle they often offer a greater selection (i.e., extended depth) than are offered by general merchandisers. For example, a consumer electronics retailer would fall into this category.
- *Single line speciality merchandisers* – Some retailers limit their offerings to just one product line (i.e., very narrow width), and sometimes only one product (i.e., very shallow depth). This can be seen online where a relatively small website may sell a single product such as computer gaming software. Another example may be a small jewellery store that only handles watches.

PRICING STRATEGY

Retailers can be classified based on their general pricing strategy. Retailers must decide whether their approach is to use price as a competitive advantage or to seek competitive advantage in non-price ways.

- *Discount pricing* – Discount retailers are best known for selling low priced products that have a low profit margin (i.e., price minus cost). To make profits these retailers look to sell in high volume. Typically discount retailers operate with low overhead costs by vigorously controlling operational spending on such things as real estate, design issues (e.g., store layout, website presentation), and by offering fewer services to their customers.
- *Competitive pricing* – The objective of some retailers is not to compete on price but alternatively not to be seen as charging the highest price. These retailers, who often operate in speciality markets, aggressively monitor the market to insure their pricing is competitive but they do not desire to get into price wars with discount retailers. Thus, other elements of the marketing mix (e.g., higher quality products, nicer store setting) are used to create higher value for which the customer will pay more.
- *Full price pricing* – Retailers targeting exclusive markets find such markets are far less price sensitive than mass or speciality markets. In these cases the additional value added through increased operational spending (e.g., expensive locations, more attractive design, more services) justify higher retail prices. While these retailers are likely to sell in lower volume than discount or competitive pricing retailers, the profit margins for each product are much higher.

Promotional Focus

Retailers generate customer interest using a variety of promotional technique, yet some retailers rely on certain methods more than others as their principle promotional approach.

— *Advertising* – Many retailers find traditional mass promotional methods of advertising, such as through newspapers or television, continue to be their best means for creating customer interest. Retailers selling online rely mostly on Internet advertising as their promotional method of choice.

— *Direct mail* – A particular form of advertising that many retailers use for the bulk of their promotion is direct mail – advertising through postal mail. Using direct mail for promotion is the primary way catalogue retailers distribute their materials and is often utilised by smaller local companies who promote using postcard mailings.

— *Personal selling* – Retailers selling expensive or high-end products find a considerable amount of their promotional effort is spent in person-to-person contact with customers. While many of these retailers use other promotional methods, in particular advertising, the consumer-salesperson relationship is key to persuading consumers to make purchase decisions.

Distribution Method

Retailers sell in many different formats with some requiring consumers visit a physical location while others sell to customers in a virtual space. It should be noted that many retailers are not tied to a single distribution method but operate using multiple methods.

— *Store-based sellers* – By far the predominant method consumers use to obtain products is to acquire these by physically visiting retail outlets. Store outlets can be further divided into several categories. One key characteristic that distinguishes categories is whether retail outlets are physically connected to one or more others stores:

— *Stand-alone* – These are retail outlets that do not have other retail outlets connected.

— *Strip-shopping centre* – A retail arrangement with two or more outlets physically connected or that share physical resources (e.g., share parking lot).

— *Shopping area* – A local centre of retail operations containing many retail outlets that may or may not be physically connected but are in close proximity to each other such as a city shopping district.

— *Regional shopping mall* – Consists of a large self-contained shopping area with many connected outlets.

— *Non-store sellers* – A fast growing method used by retailers to sell products is through methods that do not have customers physically visiting a retail outlet. In fact, in many cases customers make their purchase from within their own homes.

— *Online sellers* – The fastest growing retail distribution method allows consumer to purchase products via the Internet. In most cases delivery is then handled by a third-party shipping service.

— *Direct marketers* – Retailers that are principally selling via direct methods may have a primary location that receives orders but does not host shopping visits. Rather, orders are received via mail or phone.

— *Vending* – While purchasing through vending machines does require the consumer to physically visit a location, this type of retailing is considered as non-store retailing as the vending operations are not located at the vending company's place of business.

Service Level

Retailers attract customers not only with desirable

products and affordable prices, but also by offering services that enhance the purchase experience. There are at least three levels of retail service:

- *Self-service* – This service level allows consumers to perform most or all of the services associated with retail purchasing. For some consumers self-service is considered a benefit while others may view it as an inconvenience. Self-service can be seen with: (1) self-selection services, such as online purchasing and vending machine purchases, and (2) self-checkout services where the consumer may get help selecting the product but they use self-checkout stations to process the purchase including scanning and payment.
- *Assorted-service* – The majority of retailers offer some level of service to consumers. Service includes handling the point-of-purchase transaction; product selection assistance; arrange payment plans; offer delivery; and many more.
- *Full-service* – The full-service retailer attempts to handle nearly all aspects of the purchase to the point where all the consumer does is select the item they wish to purchase. Retailers that follow a full-price strategy often follow the full-service approach as a way of adding value to a customer's purchase.

Ownership Structure

Finally, we can categorise retailers based on the ownership structure of the business.

- *Individually owned and operated* – Under this ownership structure an individual or corporate entity owns and operates one or a very small number of outlets. Single ownership of retail outlets most frequently occurs with small retail stores, though there are some cases, for instance in the automotive or furniture industries, where single ownership involves very large outlets.

— *Corporate chain* – A retail chain consists of multiple retail outlets owned and operated by a single entity all performing similar retail activities. While the number of retail outlets required to be classified as a chain has never been specified, we will assume that anyone owning more than five retail locations would be considered a chain.

— *Corporate structure* – This classification covers large retailers predominantly operating in the non-store retail arena such as online, catalogue and vending.

— *Contractually licensed and individually operated* – The contractual channel arrangement has lead to a retail ownership structure in which operators of the retail outlet are not the out-right owners of the business. Instead, the arrangement often involves a legal agreement in which the owner of the retail concept allows the operator to run the owner's business concept in exchange for financial considerations such as a percentage of revenue. This structure is most often seen in retail franchising.

RETAIL FORMATS

Now that we have presented ways in which retailers can be classified, we now use these categories to distinguish general formats or business models that best describes a retail operation. These categories are designed to identify the primary format a retailer follows. In some cases, particularly with the advent of the Internet, a retailer will be involved in more than one format.

— *Mom-and-pop* – Represent the small, individually owned and operated retail outlet. In many cases these are family-run businesses catering to the local community often with a high level of service but relatively small product selection.

- *Mass discounters* — These retailers can be either general or speciality merchandisers but either way their main focus is on offering discount pricing. Compared to department stores, mass discounters offer fewer services and lower quality products.
- *Warehouse stores* – This is a form of mass discounter that often provides even lower prices than traditional mass discounters. In addition, they often require buyers to make purchases in quantities that are greater than what can be purchased at mass discount stores. These retail outlets provide few services and product selection can be limited. Furthermore, the retail design and layout is as the name suggests, warehouse style, with consumers often selecting products off the ground from the shipping package. Some forms of warehouse stores, called warehouse clubs, require customers purchase memberships in order to gain access to the outlet.
- *Category killers* – Many major retail chains have taken what were previously narrowly focused, small speciality store concepts and have expanded them to create large speciality stores. These so-called "category killers" have been found in such speciality areas as electronic (e.g., Best Buy), office supplies (e.g., Staples) and sporting goods (e.g., Sport Authority).
- *Departmental stores* – These retailers are general merchandisers offering mid-to-high quality products and strong level of services, though in most cases these retailers would not fall into the full-service category. While departmental stores are classified as general merchandisers some carry a more selective product line.
- *Boutique* – This retail format is best represented by a small store carrying very specialised and often high-end merchandise.

— *Catalogue retailers* – Such type of retailers have built their business by having customers place orders after seeing products that appear in a mailed catalogue. Orders are then delivered by a third-party shipper.

— *e-tailers* - Possibly the most publicised retail model to evolve in the last 50 years in Western countries is the retailer that principally sells via the Internet. There are thousands of online-only retail sellers of which Amazon.com is the most famous. These retailers offer shopping convenience including being open for business all day, every day. Electronic retailers or e-tailers also have the ability to offer a wide selection of product since all they really need in order to attract orders is a picture and description of the product. That is, they may not need to have the product on-hand the way physical stores do. Instead an e-tailer can wait until an order is received from their customers before placing their own order with their suppliers. This cuts down significantly on the cost of maintaining products in-stock.

— *Franchise* – A franchise is a form of contractual channel in which one party, the franchisor, controls the business activities of another party, the franchisee. Under these arrangements, an eligible franchisee agrees to pay for the right to use the franchisor's business methods and other important business aspects, such as the franchise name. For instance, McDonalds is a well-known franchisor that allows individuals to use the McDonalds name and methods to deliver food to consumers. Payment is usually in the form of a one-time, upfront franchise fee and also on-going percentage of revenue. While the cost to the franchisee may be quite high, this form of retailing offers several advantages including: (1) allowing the franchisee to open a retail outlet that may already be known to local customers, and (2) being trained in how to operate the business, which may allow the franchisee to be successful much faster than if they attempted to start a business on their own. For the franchisor, in addition to added revenue, the franchise model allows for faster expansion since funds needed to expand the business are often supported by the franchisee's up-front franchise fee.

— *Convenience store* – As the name implies these general merchandise retailers cater to offering customers an easy purchase experience. Convenience is offered in many ways including through easily accessible store locations, small store size that allows for quick shopping, and fast checkout. The product selection offered by these retailers is very limited and pricing can be high.

— *Vending* – Within this category are automated methods for allowing consumers to make purchases and quickly acquire products. While most consumers are well aware of vending machines allowing customers to purchase smaller items, such as beverages and snack food, newer devices are entering the market containing more expensive and bulkier products. These systems require the vending machine have either Internet or telecommunications access to permit purchase using credit cards. This method is popular in Western countries.

2

DYNAMIC NATURE OF RETAILING

Retailing is a way of life with boundless opportunities:

- Downtown areas are re-emerging as viable places to shop.
- Malls and strip centres that offer competitive leases abound.
- States are adopting financing packages designed to help businesses get started and stay open.
- More merchant organizations than ever can help the new retailer compete in the marketplace.
- And the Internet not only offers valuable retail business information and opportunities, but it also allows you to market to and communicate with your customers at virtually no cost.

Today's retailing world is made up of people with many different talents, skills, and approaches. The new kids on the block don't always have the finest college education, nor do they always come from major cities of the world. But in the retailing world, ordinary men and women can become extraordinary. The new kids can either push the established and already successful stores to become better, or they can put those old stores out of business. Great stores (big or small) thrive, and there's plenty of room for great stores.

SETTING UP A RETAIL BUSINESS

The essence of retailing is buying something and re-selling it for a profit. What you sell, where you sell it, how you price and display it, and who you sell it to are all factors that help make retailing an extremely interesting challenge.

The old retail business expression "Retail is detail" is as true today (or more so) as it was 50 years ago. And as bright new entrepreneurs enter the retail arena, each one brings a new detail to retail — a new wrinkle in the way to do business. Retailing is about creativity, and if you like change, you will love the *retail business.* In fact, creativity is the giant-slayer of businesses that are too set in their ways to change.

But while retailing can be a lot of fun, if you want your business to succeed, you need to make sure that you've tightened a few serious nuts and bolts. To help you do this, here's a handy to-do list of the basic steps you must take to create a successful retail business:

1. *Plan your business.* First, develop a business plan that forces you to document every aspect of your business. Early in the planning stage, define what kind of business you want to open and what's going to make you special, what kind of merchandise you want to carry, and what type of customers you want to attract. You must also decide where to locate your business for optimal success and how to design your store to make it attractive to customers. And before you get too far in your planning, make sure that you determine the structure of your business and obtain the necessary permits and registrations.
2. *Validate your ideas.* Ask everyone you know what he or she thinks about your idea for a new retail business. Show these people your business plan,

but be prepared for negative feedback — even your family members or closest friends will often give you the classic, "It will never work." No matter. You must ask their opinions — they may bring up some important points that you've overlooked. If anyone succeeds in talking you out of your new venture, your conviction wasn't strong enough to make it work in the first place. Now is the time to talk to as many professionals as possible. Contact your local state retail association and the trade show or association that services your industry. Many of these groups can refer you to people who will give you an honest opinion. Obviously, now is also the time to share your business plans with your friendly banker. Even if you don't need to borrow money, showing her your plans won't hurt. After your plans have been validated by the appropriate authorities, it's time to execute them (the plans, not the authorities!).

3. *Execute your plan.* Being successful requires more than just having a great idea. Lots of people have great ideas, but not many of them know how to market and execute their plans. As the ad copy said, "It's NOT how many ideas you have, it's how many ideas you can make happen."
4. *Orchestrate your grand opening.* Your next goal is to open the store. You must set two dates: one for the "soft" opening and the other for the big splash. For the soft opening, simply open the doors to your business, and whoever comes in, comes in. Taking this step gives you a chance to work out the bugs before your grand opening event that includes the ribbon-cutting, the opening party, and the grand opening sale. No matter how hard you try, preparations usually aren't complete by opening day, and opening a store that is so unready that it

looks unprofessional is the kiss of death for any new business. Your grand opening may be short term in duration, but its effect can last forever.

5. *Create your routine.* During your first year, you will establish the way your business does things — your policies and procedures. Are they working in practice? Keep a pad of paper by your cash register, and every time you think about a better way to do something, document it. As your business grows, this habit will become an invaluable tool.
6. *Grow your business.* When the newness of the experience starts to wear off and the startup phase is complete, it's time to focus on growing your business. You must now concentrate on advertising, building your brand, buying the right merchandise, and attracting the right personnel. To maintain your success, you must master the art of selling. And in order for your business to stay afloat, you must keep on top of its finances.

DECIDING IF RETAIL IS RIGHT FOR YOU

So, is the retail business right for you? If the answer is "yes," retail is right up your alley. The following questions can help you think more deeply about whether or not retail is for you:

— *Do I like to sell?* Retailing is selling! But don't worry, the days of turning the customer upside down and shaking him till the money comes out are over. Your advertising, your displays, and the contact you have with your customers are all part of the selling process. If the idea of selling scares you, beware. Retailing is selling — no matter how you disguise it.

— *Do I like to buy?* Part of retailing is shopping. If you find shopping to be a pain, you better find yourself a good buyer — or you better not go into the retail business. You have to know what your competition is doing. You're not looking to steal their ideas, but their ideas can certainly inspire some great ones of your own.

— *Do I like dealing with and serving people?* Retailing is a people business. As a retailer, you must deal with emotions both high and low. Many times, you must deal with irrational people, rationally. If you welcome this challenge, you may be right for retail.

— *Do I like to network?* Retailing is establishing contacts. When I ask myself what made me successful, I realize that I couldn't have made it without all my business contacts who've helped me over the years. Through them, I can find out which merchandise is selling and which has "slowed up," who has the best buys, and where the best seminars are. My contacts are also there for me when I get a little down in the dumps. Sometimes it's nice to have a friend around.

— *Can I motivate people?* Retailing is motivating your staff. Can you inspire your employees to man the ship and get things done when you're not around? If so, not only can you be a successful retailer, but you may also have the ability to own multiple stores — perhaps even an entire chain! The ability to motivate others is a skill that winners have.

— *Do I mind sacrificing my schedule to accommodate my customers?* Retailing isn't a Monday through Friday, 9-to-5 job. You must be in the store when your customers are there — you have to be present when and where the action is. Don't worry, you can still have a normal life and schedule — it's just that your normal will be a little different.

- *Do I like to plan?* Retailing is planning. You must plan your buying trips and what you will buy on these trips. You must plan your budget. Plan your staff. Plan when to change your displays. Plan your time on the selling floor. Get the picture? Planning is just part of the business.
- *Do I like to master new things?* Retailing is constant learning. It doesn't take place in the classroom, but when attending trade shows, looking at merchandise, listening to sales people, going to seminars and workshops, and reading trade publications. You must keep up with what's happening in your industry. There is nothing worse than a stale retailer.
- *Do I like displaying, arranging, and changing merchandise to make it look appealing enough to buy?* Retailing is displaying your merchandise in the most attractive way possible. The ability to arrange a selling floor to make the merchandise say "Buy me!" is one of the most valuable talents a retailer can have. If you don't possess this ability, find someone to do it for you.
- *Do I know (or can I master) some basic accounting to understand how I'm doing financially?* I know what you're thinking: "I'll have my accountant handle that." Sorry to tell you this, but there are a few basics that you yourself must commit to do weekly and monthly. It's not that bad, so don't get nervous — just accept the fact that you must master a few basic accounting skills.

If most of these questions excited you, you will make a great retailer. If, as you read them, you thought, "I can do that," you have retail in your blood. If you think that having some old fixtures from a store that closed and knowing a company that can supply you with some merchandise are good enough reasons to go into the retail business, think again.

REASONS FOR OPENING A STORE

Often, people open stores for the wrong reasons. What are your reasons? Are they valid? And just what is a valid reason, anyway? After all, what's right for one person may not be right for another. The following list gives some common reasons for opening a store:

- *Tapping into your creativity:* A store can provide an outlet for artistic expression. Every display tells a story, and the owners take painstaking efforts to make sure that it's perfect in every way. These retailers don't necessarily like dealing with the finicky nature of a customer – but their displays act as silent sales people that consistently make the registers ring. Those who love what they do and who work hard almost always succeed.
- *Interacting with people:* Opening a store can give you the opportunity to interact with customers and meet plenty of new people. People who open stores for this reason thrill to the challenge of developing new customers. Many don't even work for the money – some are even semiretired, but the prospect of turning a "looker" into a "buyer" is enough incentive for them to open a store.
- *Relishing the excitement:* Having a store can provide you with the excitement of buying the merchandise for it. Wielding the buying power and having access to the latest merchandise is a thrill. Wouldn't everyone love to attend the electronics or toy show in Trade Fairs. Of course they would – it's fun! There's nothing more exciting than the rush of a successful grand opening or a great promotion. *And it's fun to run a store.*

- *Creating a job for yourself:* If you are a manufacturer or a designer, opening a store can enable you to sell your merchandise directly to the public. In this way, you can create a visibility for your product that may not have been possible through the traditional channels. Or if, like the immigrants during the early part of the 20th century, you're finding it difficult to get a job, opening a store can be a way around this obstacle. Many immigrants who opened their own small retail shops went on to become the giants of the retail industry.
- *Taking the reins:* For those who have worked in retail their entire lives, opening a store can fulfil their dreams of owning their own business. These people already know the ins and outs of retailing and only need to master the backroom functions. In my opinion, this is one of the best reasons to open a store.
- *Making money:* Running a store can and should make you money — in many cases lots of it — while keeping you close to home. Many people who started with very little have gone on to make millions in the retail business. That statement is even truer today because of the effects of the Internet on retailing.

The reasons to open a store are many, but the key is to know and recognize your own reasons. Be aware, however, that your reasons for owning a store will probably change as you are exposed to more aspects of the retail business. And they will probably change as your life situation evolves. For example, a person originally opened a store because he needed to support his family but had a problem finding a job. He ended up staying in the retail business until he is fit — not because she still couldn't find a job, but because he loved the excitement of the buy and the thrill of the sale.

USING THE "8-POINT RETAIL FILTER"

So, if you've determined that you want to go forward with setting up a retail business, you're going to need some specific success strategies. This filter is a list of the eight basic elements of running a retail business. Unless every area is running efficiently, your business will have problems. On the other hand, if you address these eight points consistently and thoroughly, your business will succeed.

Retailers use this list to analyse the workings of their businesses; that's why it's important for you to be able to identify the eight points and use them to evaluate your business. The 8-Point Retail Filter helps you understand the retail business, focus on the details of retail, and set goals to bring your business to the next level. Be sure to sift every retail decision through this filter.

- *Product:* As you probably guessed, this is the stuff that your store sells. What kind of product will your store carry? Are there any special lines of this product that you'd like to carry in the future?
- *Presentation:* This is what your store looks like, inside and out. Don't fall into the trap of just letting this aspect of your store "happen." What feeling will your store's atmosphere convey? How will you display your product?
- *Procedures:* This is how your store is run. Over the years, innovative procedures have produced revolutionary concepts that have changed the face of retail. How will you do the everyday things you do? How will technology and the Internet affect the way you get things done? What goals will you work toward in this area?
- *Pricing:* This is how much you sell your product for. Will your store be a discount store, a premium

price business, or something in between? How often will you have sales?

- *Promotion:* This is how your store advertises and markets itself to the public. How are you going to tell the world you exist? Will you have nonsale promotions, as well as price promotions?
- *Profitability:* This is how much money you make from selling your product. Don't leave this item to your accountant – it could put you out of business. When do you plan on turning a profit, and will you be drawing a salary? What system will you use to remain informed of your profitability?
- *People:* This is the staff you hire to do everything from sweeping the floors to ringing up the cash register to filing your taxes. Your success depends on the team you put together. Who will you hire, and what will their roles be? Who will train your staff?
- *Brand:* This is how your store distinguishes itself from others like it. Brand often plays a major role in why a customer chooses one store over another. What will customers associate your store with? How will you promote your brand?

3

TYPES OF RETAIL OUTLETS

A specialist store or a small local store may have a very intimate relationship with its customers, with transactions being made on a face-to-face, first name basis. At the other end of the scale, goods may be retailed across the globe, with no physical contact being made at all.

CLOTHING AND ACCESSORY STORE

Products

Clothing and accessory stores sell apparel for all members of the family, as well as luggage, leather goods, lingerie, jewellery, uniforms, and bridal gowns. Stores in this sector may sell all of the above items or concentrate on a few.

Expertise

Clothing and accessory stores are often staffed with knowledgeable salespersons who can help in the selection of sizes, styles, and accessories.

DEPARTMENTAL STORE

Departmental stores sell a wide selection of merchandise

with no one line predominating. These stores generally are arranged into departments with a manager heading each department.

Products

Departmental stores may sell apparel, furniture, appliances, home furnishings, cosmetics, jewellery, paint, hardware, electronics, and sporting goods. They may also sell food and services such as optical, photography, pharmacy, insurance and travel brokerage. They are the ultimate one-stop shop.

Discount Departmental Stores

Discount departmental stores typically have fewer sales workers, relying more on self-service features, and have centrally located cashiers. Departmental stores that sell bulk items, like major appliances, usually provide delivery and installation services. Upscale departmental stores may offer tailoring for their clothing lines and more personal services.

DISTANCE RETAILING

Rather than visiting a store to make a purchase, a customer may order products from a remote location. This may be done by mail, telephone, internet/email or other digital device such as interactive television and even from a refrigerator.

Physical Stores *v* Virtual Stores

Retailers that practice distance retailing may also have physical stores, such as Reliance. Others may not, such as True value stores.

Products

All manner of products can be sold in this way, from

food groceries and large items like beds, that are usually delivered by dedicated vehicles, to many smaller non-food items that tend to be delivered by a courier or by parcel mail, such as fly killers. The range of products on offer is only limited by the budget of the customer and the shipping infrastructure available in a given region.

Advantages of Distance Retailing

The customer does not need to travel to the store in order to purchase goods, saving time and travel costs. Browsing through different catalogues or on the internet or mobile phone can also save a lot of time compared with travelling from store to store.

Disadvantages of Distance Retailing

There are certain products that customers prefer to touch, feel and even try out before they purchase. An example of this is clothing. There is, however, a distinction to be made between different types of distance selling. For example, music can be sampled on the internet or some mobile phones but this cannot be done with printed catalogues.

Some customers are uncomfortable purchasing goods at a distance if the seller isn't known to them. Whilst local stores will develop a word-of-mouth reputation in the community, it is harder to poll opinions for stores that are far away.

DOOR-TO-DOOR RETAILING

This kind of retailing is as old as retailing itself and is still very common, although less so in recent times. A door-to-door salesperson may be self-employed or employed by a company and will usually specialise in a particular product group, often household items. Although it is common for them to visit houses, they may also sell to businesses.

Area of Coverage

Door-to-door sales people can be split into two main groups. The first group are those that stay in one locality, selling to regular customers. Fruits and Vegetables or fresh meat, eggs, bread etc. sales are typically made by these local sales people. They will have regular "rounds" and will try to time their visit so that they appear at a given location at the same time each day. This way, customers may come to depend on them. The local door-to-door salesperson may also try to extend their round to take in more customers.

The second group are travelling sales people. They may procure goods in a more opportunist way, taking advantage of a bargain when it comes along, or buying goods to coincide with environmental changes or particular events in the calendar. For instance, such a salesperson may sell warm clothes at the onset of cold weather but also sell gifts at festive times. Once they have sold their goods, or reached the point where they have few customers left to sell to, they will move to another area and repeat the process. As well as buying goods to sell on, they may also sell goods that they have made themselves or that their family or community have made. They also may provide services to customers, such as mending, sewing, light maintenance, knife sharpening etc.

Advantages

One advantage of being a door-to-door salesperson is that the overheads are relatively low. Some door-to-door sales people will carry all of their stock on a vehicle but others may store it in their homes or a small warehouse (sometimes known as a "lock up"). They can also be flexible in the range that they can carry. This can allow them to be very up-to-date with the products that they can offer.

Disadvantages

Disadvantages include the lack of security in travelling door-to-door whilst carrying a high value of stock or money. Another disadvantage is that where a shop's customers come to the shop, door-to-door sales people spend a lot of valuable time and often transport costs visiting their customers — and there is no guarantee of a sale.

CHAINS

If a store is successful, this will often encourage the owner or owners to attempt to repeat the success and open a similar store elsewhere. Thus, a chain of stores is established. Where a store chain comprises a few stores, it is very common for members of an extended family to run them.

Non-Franchised Chain

Structure

Each store in a chain (or multiple store) is called a branch. The original store, or the most important store, may double as the head office. Very large chains may have a completely separate building as their head office.

The way chain stores are managed can vary from a centrally controlled operation at one extreme where virtually all decisions are made by the head office, to the other extreme where each store can be run as a mini business and simply return a profit to the centre. It is very common for chain store management arrangements to be somewhere in between these extremes, where smaller scale and local decisions are made by the branches and decisions affecting the whole chain are made by the head office.

Economies of Scale

As the chain grows in size and total sales volumes increase, the company managing the chain is able to purchase goods for the stores at terms that are more favourable. They can also exert more influence over the attributes of the goods they buy and sell such as the sourcing, the products' features, the packaging they come in and even the distribution and logistics involved in getting them to the stores.

Other benefits also arise, such as rationalising some management tasks across the whole chain and having uniform procedures and systems common to all of the stores. They can also rationalise marketing across the chain. This not only is more efficient, it also allows marketing messages to be more potent. An example of a non-franchised chain is Reliance.

Franchise Store Chain

Some companies will concentrate their resources on marketing their brand rather than developing a chain of stores. The marketing creates demand for the brand, which may be a group of unique products or may be a unique sales format. The founding company will then franchise others to open their own stores and to sell the brand. The company that establishes the franchise operation is the franchisor. The storekeeper is the franchisee.

Symbiotic arrangement

This can be a symbiotic arrangement because the franchisor has a sales outlet for its brand and the franchisee benefits from the marketing and/or part-exclusivity of selling a unique brand.

Exclusivity

Often the franchisee is restricted to purchasing the brand exclusively from the franchisor.

Franchisor Control

The purchase of point of sale material and shop fixtures will also be under the direction of the franchisor in many cases, and the design of the store and the methods and procedures carried out by the staff may also be under the franchisor's instruction.

Some franchises are so valuable that the franchisor can charge money just for a license to open a franchise outlet before any trading has taken place.

PARTY AND EVENT RETAILING

This is usually a form of franchising where the retailer invites people from the locality to a common location. The event or the party will be a mix of socialising and retailing, usually themed around the products on offer. Most commonly, the retailer will be a franchisee to a wider organisation.

Products

Although party and event selling can involve a variety of goods, it is very common that cosmetics, small household goods, clothing and etc. are sold.

Low Cost

Party selling is common throughout the world and can be a low cost way of retailing for both the franchisor and franchisee.

Samples

Often the franchisor will supply samples and a small

selection of goods to the franchisee so that their potential customers at the event can try the products out.

Recruitment

These parties can also be used to recruit new franchisees.

SINGLE INDEPENDENT NON-FRANCHISED STORE

A single independent store may be run an individual, but is more typically run by a family.

Decline

In highly industrialised regions, these types of outlets have decreased in number, in favour of franchise operations or chains.

Products and Catchment

They may be general stores, catering to a limited geographical range or may sell specialised products to a wider area.

Pros and Cons

The advantages of single independent stores are that they can be tailored to their customers needs and offer a more personal service. One of the main disadvantages is that the running costs may not be as favourable as with a chain or franchise. If the store is selling general goods, the costs of purchasing stock will also be higher.

STREET MARKET

The tradition of selling from market stalls goes back to the early days of retailing where traders could gather in one area to sell their wares. It is very popular retailing.

Location

Street markets, or open-air markets, are common around

the world and are particularly popular in temperate or warm climates.

Regulation

In many countries, street trading has been increasingly regulated through history. In England, towns were given rights by the King or Queen of the day to hold a market. These charters specified the nature of the market and laid down the days when it could operate. Some towns had a permanent market while others were permitted to hold their market just one or two days in the week such as Som Bazar, Mangal Bazar etc.

Types of Street Market Retailer

Street market traders can be put into two categories, (*i*) those that sell goods opportunistically, taking advantages of low cost goods that come available, or environmental and other conditions that temporarily increase demand for particular products; (*ii*) those that regularly sell one product type to regular customers.

Governance

The way that street markets are operated and governed vary. The following variations are possible, including a mix of some of them:

1. *No formal governance. Traders* will simply share a space along a road (or an off-street area) and trade as separate businesses. This type of arrangement has little or no bureaucracy and can be very efficient for the traders. Often traders will not pay any rent for their space (or "pitch"). Many traders will keep their pitch for many years, even handing their "right" to this space from generation to generation. Although it can be advantageous to the incumbent stall holders, this can lead to a lowering of competition as new stall holders find it difficult

to come onto the market. Occasionally this informal arrangement can lead to gangsterism and even violence between stall holders and with potential stall holders. It could also give rise to protection rackets and other illegal activity.

2. *Council run:* Street markets are commonly run by local civic authorities, who set the regulations and, where appropriate charge rental fees. The regulations can range from informal arrangements involving the allocation of street area only to very strict regulations with an enforcement regime where traders may be inspected regularly for health and safety and other legal requirements and may be restricted to selling certain types of goods. As well as renting plots of land, some civic authorities may even rent the stalls themselves, which may be permanent fixtures on a street (or off-street area).
3. *Run by a company:* A company may own or rent a street (or an off-street area) and, in turn, rent small plots of land to stallholders. They may also impose regulations in a similar way that civic authorities do. Some companies such as large retailers, may have a street market on their forecourt or other area that they own. Good street markets can attract many shoppers. A retailer may find that having a market outside their bricks and mortar store may be good for their trade. They may charge a low rent or no rent at all in order to encourage stall holders to trade on their land and to keep their prices low, thereby attracting more customers. They, may, however, restrict stall holders to selling goods that do not compete with their own products, subject to competition laws that may exist in the jurisdiction.
4. *Run by a co-operative (Co-op):* The stallholders themselves may own or rent the land on which

their stalls are trading. They may contribute towards the costs of maintaining or paying for the site by each paying an amount of money. The amount paid may simply be commensurate with the amount of stalls they own, or may be linked to the amount of turnover they can achieve or may be negotiated on a stallholder-by-stallholder basis. It is common for street trader co-ops to have regulations that are binding on each member. Once again, these regulations may range from a few informal rules to detailed and specific rules. Many co-ops will operate a democratic system whereby they may elect a leader, or a council (or both) to run the co-op, or may even vote on every decision.

Pros and Cons

The advantages of street market retailing are that it has relatively low overheads and allows flexibility. The disadvantages are that sales can be adversely affected in inclement weather and the stall (usually) needs to be set up each day, which can take a considerable amount of time and effort. There also needs to be an area for goods to be stored when the stall is not being used.

SUPERMARKET

A supermarket is "a large self-service grocery store selling groceries and dairy products and household goods". In addition the word "supermarket" means different things to different countries around the world, as global supermarket chains have discovered recently. From the beginnings of the retail trade there has been a trend for general stores to increase in size and for specialist stores to combine. It is believed that store chains have existed from as early as 2,200 years ago; the first self-service store was first introduced in 1916 in the United States. So, all the elements of the supermarket were in place.

In the absence of a universal definition for the supermarket there can be no authoritative reference point in history that marks the shift from small general stores to supermarkets. There are, however, important milestones, such as the growth of The Great Atlantic & Pacific Tea Company, which, in 1910 opened the Economy Store format, selling basic dry groceries such as tea, coffee and tinned foods. These items were sold in relatively high volume at low margin, another hallmark of the supermarket. They also only traded in ready cash and generally did not allow credit nor delivery to customers. This "cash and carry" concept grew rapidly over the coming years.

After the introduction of self-service in 1916, and despite the recession that followed in the 1920's, many stores continued to consolidate and increase their sales volumes, thus improving their efficiency and buying power. The next two milestone were the introduction of faster means of transport, especially the motor vehicle, and the rapid take-up of home refrigerators. These two elements allowed more affluent consumers to require larger quantities of food in one shopping trip. As this one-stop-shop tendency spread throughout the Western countries, shopkeeper and store chains became increasingly aware of the critical need to attract these customers to their stores. This resulted in the lower prices, but also drove these companies to try new ideas such as the Drive-In store. As these stores were specifically for car users, they did not need to be situated in the expensive centre of town but instead were typically found in lower rent neighbourhoods on the outskirts.

Although the drive-in concept was short-lived, the idea of accommodating cars may have been the final piece of the jigsaw. By combining car-parking, self-service, low prices with high volumes, the supermarket concept began in earnest in the 1930's in the U.S. All these elements were brought together in the mind of Michael J. Cullen who suggested to his employers, Mutual Grocery and Kroger Stores, that they open a very large store on the outskirts of town selling national brands at low margin. His idea wasn't taken up by his bosses, so he decided to open his own store in a vacant garage in Jamaica Avenue, Long Island, Queens in New York. Its sheer size prompted customers to call it a "warehouse grocery store". To make this a true one-stop shop, Cullen had concessionaires retailing those goods that the store wouldn't ordinarily sell. This store, and the chain that followed, was enormously successful and was soon followed by many others.

These stores not only attracted affluent car owners. The U.S. was in a recession and the low prices on offer attracted many poorer customers who would travel the extra distance in order to benefit from the savings they made on basic goods and the chance to buy items they otherwise could not afford.

VAN RETAILING

This is a cross between door-to-door sales and store sales. The retailer will typically keep 1 day's stock in their van and visit an area where they will service regular customers. They may occasionally visit an area that they do not usually go to in order to attract new customers. Van sales are common in rural areas and in less developed economies.

Static *v* Roving

There are two types of van sales. One is where the van is parked in a common area and is visited by customers; ices and snacks are often sold this way. The other type of van sales is, in effect, the same as door-to-door selling. This is where the retailer uses the van to travel from house to house, selling to customers on their doorstep and using the van as a means to hold and carry stock.

Products

The kinds of products sold from vans tend to be everyday items such as cleaning products. Snack foods and ices may also be sold from vans. Vans specifically designed to work at a very low temperature may specialise in frozen food sales.

Regulation

In some states, the area that van sales can cover and the products that can be sold may be subject to regulations and may require licensing.

"Van Wars"

Occasionally there are disputes between van sales competitors especially when they are competing in the same area.

CHOOSING A TYPE OF RETAIL BUSINESS

Entrepreneurs have many forms of retail business ownership available to them. Each business model has its own list of pros and cons. Choosing a type of retail business to start will depend on why you want to own a business, as well as your lifestyle, family, personality, basic skills and much more. Here are a few of the main types of retail ownership and the advantages, disadvantages, and support system of each.

Independent Retailer

An independent retailer is one who builds his/her business from the ground up. From the business planning stage to opening day, the independent retail owner does it all. He/she may hire consultants, staff and others to assist in the business endeavour. The opportunities are endless.

Advantages

There are no restrictions on who, how or where an entrepreneur should set up his/her business. The freedom to do what one wants to do is the biggest advantage in this form of business. It can be extremely fulfilling.

Disadvantages

Because of the ease and flexibility of getting started, there can be a lot of competition in a particular area for a certain type of customer. Every business decision rests on the owner(s). There is no branding, no preset guidelines and a great deal of risk in this business model.

Support

Other than small business resources online, in print or sponsored by the various government and trade organisations, there isn't much in the way of support for the independent retailer.

Taking Over An Existing Retail Business

Someone who inherits or buys an existing business is taking ownership and responsibility of someone else's hard work. The foundation has already been laid.

Advantages

The biggest advantage to buying an existing business or taking ownership of an already-established retail store is time. The time to build a customer base, the time to establish branding, and the time it takes to establish credit are generally all past which means most of the hard part is behind the new owner.

Disadvantages

The existing business may have a negative image or

reputation that will take a lot of time to undo. Loyal customers may not like the change of ownership. Previous owners have caused problems by opening a competing business.

Support

A well-established business will usually have a written set of procedures or policy manual. Staff members already in place have the knowledge to help guide a new owner.

Franchises

Purchasing a franchise is buying the right to use a name, product, concept and business plan. The franchisee will receive a proven business model from an established business.

Advantages

All of the business operation processes have been established. The franchisee receives help from a network and customers may already familiar with the name. The marketing strategy has already been put in place. Most all of the risk associated with starting a retail business has been reduced.

Disadvantages

Franchisees pay a fee, or royalty, based on sales each year. Startup costs relating to the franchise may be high. One of the biggest disadvantages of owning a franchise is the lack of flexibility and freedom.

Support

Franchisors usually provide all the marketing, training and on-going support needed to run a successful business.

4

STARTING A RETAIL BUSINESS

STEPS TO STARTING A RETAIL BUSINESS

The dream of starting a retail business can easily become a reality. It may take a lot of initial work as you start your own business, but with the right planning anyone can achieve their goals. Starting a retail business, the following steps should be used as a guide before you open a store.

Choose a Business Legal Structure

Choosing the proper legal organisational structure for your business is one of the most important decisions you will make. While it is possible to change your structure at a later date, it can be a difficult and expensive process. Therefore it's better to make the right decision before you start your own business.

Choose a Name for Your Retail Business

Dreaming up a moniker may come easy for some, but others struggle with the task. Here are some do's and don'ts for naming your own retail business.

Decide What Products to Sell

Finding a product for your retail business to sell may

very well be the most difficult decision you will need to make when starting a retail business. Before you commit to a product or product line, consider these factors while deciding what to resell.

Write a Business Plan

Whether it is formal or informal, on paper or on disk, the process of creating a business plan will only help your business become successful. It is one of the most crucial steps in starting a retail business. Learn how to write a business plan for your retail store, why writing a business plan is necessary, purchase business plan software and view free sample retail business plans.

Learn the Laws

Understand what business licenses and permits you need to obtain by contacting your city, and state government offices. Before you start your own business, find out what laws govern your type of retail store. Consider consulting with both a lawyer and an accountant, as each will help you properly organise your business.

Find a Location

Where you choose to locate your retail business will have a major impact on everything your shop does. The difference between selecting the wrong location and the right site could be the difference between business failure and success.

Buy Wholesale Products to Resell

A successful retail business depends greatly on offering the right product, at the right price, at the right time. Therefore, it is paramount to the success of your business to be able to locate the best sources for those products. As you take this step to starting a retail business and decide what products or product lines you would like to sell, it's then time to find places to buy those items at wholesale.

Establish Store Policies

The best time to establish policies and procedures for your retail business is during the planning stages. By anticipating problems before you open your doors, you can choose how you'll handle special situations, as well as the normal day to day operations. This helps avoid making mistakes once you're faced with customers.

Spread the Word

Before you open a retail store, start spreading the word. Create a retail marketing plan, brainstorm sales promotion ideas, begin branding and advertising your retail store.

CHOOSE A BUSINESS LEGAL STRUCTURE

Choosing the proper legal organisational structure for your business is one of the most important decisions you will make. While it may not have much impact on the day-to-day operations of a small business, it can have a huge impact come tax time, when you want to borrow money or attract investors, or in the unfortunate event you get taken to court. While it is possible to change your structure at a later date, it can be a difficult and expensive process. Better to make the right decision in the first place.

There are numerous books and other products available to help you do the filings yourself, as well as many Internet services that will do them for you. However, depending on the size and complexity of your business, you may want to consult with an attorney, and you almost certainly should consult with your tax advisor regarding which structure is best for your situation.

The following are the basic forms of business ownership.

Sole Proprietorship

The individual owner of an unincorporated business operates the business as an extension of himself. The profits and losses of the business are reported on the tax return of the owner - there is no separate business filing. The owner is personally responsible for any liabilities of the business. If someone sues the business for breach of contract, personal injury, or to collect a debt, the court can directly levy the personal bank account and other property of the owner. The major advantage of sole proprietorship is that it is the simplest and least expensive structure, as there is really nothing to set up and maintain.

General Partnership

Two or more people own the business jointly and share profits and losses of the business as spelled out in the partnership agreement. Each partner is potentially responsible for the full amount of all liabilities of the business, i.e., a creditor can collect the full amount of a debt of the partnership from the partner that is the easiest to collect from. Distribution of profits and losses is determined by the partnership agreement and passes through to the individual partners. It does not have to match the ownership percentages. The partnership itself is not subject to any income or franchise tax. Control of the business is determined by the partnership agreement, but unless stated otherwise, the partners control the business jointly, with each partner having an equal vote. An advantage of partnerships is that, like a sole proprietorship, no state filings are required to create the business entity, nor are there any ongoing reporting requirements.

Limited Partnership

The basic structure and tax implications are the same as for a general partnership, but the limited partnership allows for one or more limited partners, or "silent partners", to own a portion of the business, but not participate in the management of the business. The partnership must also have a general partner who has personal liability for all liabilities of the partnership. This structure allows a partnership to have outside investors without subjecting them to the liabilities of the business.

CHOOSE A NAME FOR YOUR RETAIL BUSINESS

Creating a business name is easily one of the most enjoyable, yet utterly important, aspects of starting a retail business. Coming up with business name ideas may come easy for some, but others struggle with the task. The wrong business name can actually be the end of a well-built business plan. Let's use brainstorming to generate some solid business name ideas.

Business Name Do's and Don'ts

Keep these tips in mind while choosing your new business name:

- Do make it easy to understand, spell and pronounce.
- Don't use negative sounding words.
- Do consider where your business will fall in an alphabetical list such as the yellow pages.
- Don't limit your product line by choosing a name that won't represent all you do.
- Do create a name you can stand behind.

- Don't use a strictly generic term, such as 'discount office supply' which cannot be protected as trademarks.
- Do be creative and imaginative.

DECIDE WHAT PRODUCTS TO SELL

Choosing a product for your retail store to sell may very well be the most difficult decision you will need to make when starting a retail business. The choices are limitless and the task may be overwhelming at first. Not only should there be a demand for your products, but it must be profitable and something you enjoy selling. Before you commit to a product or product line, consider the following factors while deciding what products to sell.

Marketability

Let's face it, it won't matter what products you sell if your customers aren't buying. Before considering what product to sell, determine what market you want to sell to. Once you know what kind of customer you want, then you'll be able to determine their needs. If your products only appeal greatly to some people, it may not be enough to sustain a business. Your product selection doesn't have to appeal to all of the population but it should be something you can convince a large percentage of shoppers they need.

Profit Margin

Selling big items is generally more profitable, but can require more credibility to sell. When you look at the price of the product, don't forget to calculate direct and indirect costs of selling your goods. The best selling products won't ever earn any real money if your margin is too small.

Consumable

Choose a product with recurring sales value. A consumable item that needs to be replaced on a regular basis is one way a retailer can establish long term sales. By establishing a customer base with recurring products, customers will continue to come back to you to buy more as they use up the products. Additionally, satisfied customers are more open to recommendations for related products.

What's Popular

When it comes to selecting products to sell based on what's popular, timing is extremely important. New trends and products can be a great boost to your business but you'll need to be at the beginning of the product lifecycle in order to be successful. Learning to pick a hot product before it becomes hot is a valuable skill that comes from knowing your market.

Competition

Competition is healthy and there are ways other than volume and price a smaller store can compete with larger retailers. On the other hand, the more unique the product, the less chance of competition.

Private Label

One way to guarantee having a truly unique product line is to make the item yourself. Another way is to partner with a small business that makes a product you would enjoy selling. Also consider private label products which will allow you to brand an item made by another person.

Quality

When deciding which products to sell in your store, ask yourself the following question. Is this product something

I would give my dearest friend? If not, you may want to keep looking. Product quality is extremely important when your reputation is on the line.

Diversity

Keep your product offering simple in the beginning. If your product line is narrow and focused, then your marketing efforts can be just as tightly focused, which will bring you the best results for your marketing dollars. As your business grows, so can your product line as long as you keep new products compatible with the type of business, your location and your market.

Some questions to keep in mind while selecting products for resale.

- Would you buy it and use it yourself?
- Can you see yourself getting excited about this product or service?
- Would you sell it to someone you know?
- Is there a real need for the product in today's market?
- Can you imagine yourself selling this item for the next several?

The key to having a successful business is to know your products and to believe in the merchandise that you are selling. If you do not believe in the product yourself, then you probably won't be successful at selling it. Keep brainstorming and you'll find a product or product line that meets both the needs of your target market and your own ability to locate it, purchase it and resell it.

WRITE A BUSINESS PLAN FOR RETAIL STORE

One of the most important things you can do for your business, new or existing, is to write a business plan. Businesses have different reasons to write a business plan but the process of creating a business plan will only help the business become successful. Before beginning to write a business plan, research your market and gather current industry data. Retailers will find a variety of official statistics for the industry, general demographic information, polls, trends, and other retail analysis online.

Sample Plans and Software

A business plan for a retail store can be a complex multi-page document created using special software or it can be a page torn from a notebook. Whatever format is used, be sure to include the essential parts of a retail business plan. If you're having trouble writing a business plan or need help creating a format, download a free business plan template, get sample business plans, or use a business plan outline to get started writing your business plan.

There are various business plan software packages on the market today. Most of the business plan programmes provide document templates, free sample plans and advice for writing a business plan.

Learn the Laws

Knowing what licenses and permits your retail business needs can be very confusing when planning a new business. Each item requires time, energy and paperwork (depending on the government office you're dealing with) to obtain the proper registrations.

As unpleasant a task as it may be, don't risk your business shutting down before it fully begins. Conducting business without the proper licensing is a criminal offence in some states, while others hand out hefty fines. Here are some of the more common retail licenses and permits to keep your business operating legally.

Business License

How and where you register a retailing business with the state will depend on your state's laws. To find out what is needed to obtain a business license in your state, start by visiting your state's official website. You can usually find it at www.Your State's Name.gov. Most states have resources on how to register a new business and all of the requirements that must be met.

If you have a retail business located within the city limits, you may also be required to purchase a local business license. Some states and other municipalities also require a license. Call your states or city's local office for more information. The fee varies depending on the type of business and where it is located.

Business Name Registration or DBA Certificate

If you use any name for your retail business other than your own personal name, you'll need to file the appropriate paperwork. Some business licenses include a business name registration; others require a separate registration. When you file for a corporate business structure, a foreign or fictitious name application is generally included. Again, check your state's laws for more details.

Professional Licenses

Some industry-specific retailers such as auctioneers, hair dressers, pharmacists, optometrists and other professionals may require state or local occupational licenses. If you're not sure you need an occupational license, check with your industry's trade association or your state's licensing department.

Certificate of Occupancy

A certificate of occupancy may be required in some areas.

After applying, the property is inspected by representatives of the necessary agencies. These may include the fire department inspector, the building inspector and the health and/or sanitation inspector.

Other Permits

There is no way to list all required permits, as the laws and regulations vary from place to place and from industry to industry. Check with local officials to find out what permits, if any, your retail business needs. Here are a few common permits to consider.

- Alcohol and Tobacco Sales
- Alarm System Permit
- Building Construction
- Health Permit
- Signage
- Special Events
- Zoning

Before you open your doors to customers, be sure you've done the necessary research on retail business licenses and permits you need. Start filing the paperwork as soon as you can, expect delays and provide all the necessary information to avoid any problems opening your business. Consult with a business lawyer if you have any unusual circumstances or need further clarification on obtaining retailing licenses and permits.

Find a Location

Where you choose to locate your retail business will have a major impact on everything your shop does. The difference between selecting the wrong location and the right site could be the difference between business failure and success.

Before choosing a retail store location, define how you see your business, both now and in the future.

- What do your customers look like?
- Can you visualise your building?
- Do you know what you want to sell and what you want your business to be known for?
- Have you determined how much retail space, storage area, or the size of the office you need?

Without the answers to these basic questions, it will be hard to find the perfect location for generating the maximum amount of profit for your retail store.

Type of Goods

Examine what kind of products you sell, as some goods will require certain types of locations. Would your store be considered a convenience store, a specialty shop or a shopping store?

Convenience goods require easy access, allowing the customer to quickly make a purchase. A mall would not be a good location for convenience goods. This product type is lower priced and purchased by a wide range of customers.

Speciality goods are more unique than most products and customers generally won't mind travelling out of the way to purchase this type of product. This type of store may also do well near other shopping stores.

A shopping store usually sells items at a higher price which are bought infrequently by the customer. Furniture, cars and upscale clothing are examples of goods found at a shopping store. Because the prices of theses items are higher, this type of customer will want to compare prices before making a purchase. Therefore, retailers will do well to locate their store near like stores.

Population and Your Customer

If you are choosing a city or state to locate your retail store, research the area thoroughly before making a final decision. Read local papers and speak to other small businesses in the area. Obtain location demographics from the local library, chamber of commerce or the Census Bureau. Any of these sources should have information on the area's population, income and age. You know who your customers are, so make sure you find a location where your customers live, work and shop.

Accessibility, Visibility and Traffic

Don't confuse a lot of traffic for a lot of customers. Retailers want to be located where there are many shoppers but only if that shopper meets the definition of their target market. Small retail stores may benefit from the traffic of nearby larger stores.

- How many people walk or drive past the location.
- Is the area served by public transportation?
- Can customers and delivery trucks easily get in and out of the parking lot?
- Is there adequate parking?

Depending on the type of business, it would be wise to have somewhere between 5 to 8 parking spaces per 1,000 square feet of retail space.

When considering visibility, look at the location from the customer's view point. Can the store be seen from the main flow of traffic? Will your sign be easily seen? In many cases, the better visibility your retail store has, the less advertising needed. A speciality retail store located six miles out of town in a free standing building will need more marketing than a shopping store located in a mall.

Signage, Zoning and Planning

Before signing a lease, be sure you understand all the rules, policies and procedures related to your retail store location. Contact the local city hall and zoning commission for information on regulations regarding signage. Ask about any restrictions that may affect your retail operation and any future planning that could change traffic, such as highway construction.

Competition and Neighbours

Other area businesses in your prospective location can actually help or hurt your retail shop. Determine if the types of businesses nearby are compatible you're your store. For example, a high-end fashion boutique may not be successful next door to a discount variety store. Place it next to a nail or hair salon and it may do much more business.

Location Costs

Besides the base rent, consider all costs involved when choosing a retail store location.

- Who pays for lawn care, building maintenance, utilities and security?
- Who pays for the upkeep and repair of the heating/air units?
- If the location is remote, how much additional marketing will it take for customers to find you?
- How much is the average utility bill?
- Will you need to make any repairs, do any painting or remodelling to have the location fit your needs?
- Will the retailer be responsible for property taxes?

The location you can afford now and what you can afford in the future should vary. It is difficult to create sales projects on a new business, but one way to get help in determining how much rent you can pay is to find out what sales similar retail businesses are making and how much rent they're paying.

Personal Factors

If you plan to work in your store, think about your personality, the distance from the shop to home and other personal considerations. If you spend much of your time travelling to and from work, the commute may overshadow the exhilaration of being your own boss. Also, many restrictions placed on a tenant by a landlord, management company or community can hamper a retailer's independence.

Special Considerations

Your retail shop may require special considerations. Make a list of any unique characteristic of your business that may need to be addressed.

- Will the store require special lighting, fixtures or other hardware installed?
- Are restrooms for staff and customers available?
- Is there adequate fire and police protection for the area?
- Is there sanitation service available?
- Does the parking lot and building exterior have adequate lighting?
- Does the building have a canopy that provides shelter if raining?
- What is the crime rate in the area?
- Are there restrictions on Sunday sales?

Don't feel rushed into making a decision on where to put your retail store. Take your time, research the area and have patience. If you have to change your schedule and push back the date of the store's opening, than do so. Waiting to find the perfect store location is better than just settling for the first place that comes along. The wrong location choice could be devastating to your retail business.

Buy Wholesale Products to Resell

Having a successful retail business depends greatly on offering the right product, at the right price, at the right time. Therefore, it is paramount to the success of your business to be able to locate the best sources for those products. Once you know what products or product lines you would like to sell, it's time to find places to buy wholesale merchandise.

Buying Wholesale Merchandise

Before you buy wholesale merchandise for your store, try to visit a competitor or a store selling a product line similar to what you plan to sell. Browse the store's product selection, making a mental note of the brands they carry. What products seem to be selling well? Which items are in the clearance bin? If you visit a similar store too far away to be a competitor, that retailer may be willing to share with you the source of his wholesale merchandise.

Retailers can often find products to sell in their stores by searching online, joining buying groups, using library resources and attending trade shows or buyers' markets. A trade show is one of the best places to buy wholesale merchandise for your store. Retailers can find many suppliers, serving the same markets, and their product offerings. Conduct an online search for tradeshows in your industry to find the nearest event. Trade shows aren't open to the general public so be prepared to show proof that you're an established business such as license or permit.

Once your store is open and doing business, it will be easier to find wholesale merchandise to sell because the suppliers will be coming to you, instead of you looking for them. Customers can also play a large role in finding suppliers as they recommend products they would like to see in the store.

Types of Suppliers

Manufacturer—Some manufacturers will sell their products at wholesale prices directly to the retailer. If they do, they may sell their products at large quantities or at a high minimum order. If you have a particular product you want to sell, contact the manufacturer and ask if they sell directly to dealers. If not, ask what distributors they sell their products through so you will know where to buy the items.

Importers—Due to globalisation, importing products has become much easier than it used to be. Retailers can purchase from importers or buy the products directly from a foreign company. Before using this type of supplier, do your homework. It is important to understand all the aspects of the paperwork, shipping time, product life cycle and all costs involved.

Distributors—A distributor generally sells a large variety of a certain classification of products. They must make a profit too, so their prices may be slightly higher than if the item was purchased directly from the manufacturer. Retailers can buy lower quantities with little or no minimum order. Some even offer free freight on orders over a certain amount.

Other wholesalers and liquidators—In searching for products at wholesale prices, you may find wholesalers that don't sell just one type of merchandise but many, many kinds of products. Some will sell closeouts, truckloads and pallets of merchandise and even damaged goods. Before buying wholesale merchandise from this type of supplier, be sure you completely understand the condition, price and terms of the sale.

Auctions—Retailers can find many bargains on eBay, the world's largest auction site. Just browse the Wholesale Lots category of the type of store you have and you'll find tons of merchandise. Not all product prices on eBay are truly wholesale but if you spend time watching the auctions and learn how to buy effectively, you're sure to find a deal. Don't miss out on live auctions for bargains on merchandise for resale.

Choosing a Vendor

Once you've located several sources of products, evaluate each vendor on a variety of factors. In order to bring the best merchandise to your customers, you'll need to buy from someone offering quality products, reliable delivery and superior customer service. This information can be gathered through references, marketing material or by simply asking the sales representative how they conduct business.

Other Factors to Consider

- Stability
- Price
- Location
- Shipping Options
- Shipping Costs
- Customer Service
- Terms of Sale
- Business Hours
- Returned Merchandise
- Website and Online Purchasing

5

STRUCTURING YOUR RETAIL STORE

An organisational structure is a mostly hierarchical concept of subordination of entities that collaborate and contribute to serve one common aim. Organisations are a number of clustered entities. The structure of an organisation is usually set up in one of a variety of styles, dependent on their objectives and ambience. The structure of an organisation will determine the modes in which it shall operate and will perform.

Organisational structure allows the expressed allocation of responsibilities for different functions and processes to different entities. Ordinary description of such entities is as branch, site, department, work groups and single people. Contracting of individuals in an organisational structure normally is under timely limited work contracts or work orders or under timely unlimited employment contracts or programme orders.

The set organisational structure may not coincide with facts, evolving in operational action. Such divergence decreases performance, when growing. E.g. a wrong organisational structure may hamper cooperation and thus hinder the completion of orders in due time and within limits of resources and budgets. Organisational structures shall be adaptive to process requirements, aiming to optimise the ratio of effort and input to output.

An effective organisational structure shall facilitate working relationships between various entities in the organisation and may improve the working efficiency within the organisational units. Organisation shall retain a set order and control to enable monitoring the processes. Organisation shall support command for coping with a mix of orders and a change of conditions while performing work. Organisation shall allow for application of individual skills to enable high flexibility and apply creativity. When a business expands, the chain of command will lengthen and the spans of control will widen. When an organisation comes to age, the flexibility will decrease and the creativity will fatigue. Therefore organisational structures shall be altered from time to time to enable recovery. If such alteration is prevented by internal or external forces, the final escape is to turn down the organisation to prepare for a re-launch in an entirely new set up.

Common success criteria for organisational structures are:

- Decentralised reporting
- Flat hierarchy
- High transient speed
- High transparency
- Low residual mass
- Permanent monitoring
- Rapid response
- Shared reliability
- Matrix hierarchy etc.

Organisational structures developed from the ancient times of hunters and collectors in tribal organisations through highly royal and clerical power structures to industrial structures and today's post-industrial structures.

ORGANISATIONAL STRUCTURE TYPES

Pre-bureaucratic Structures

Pre-bureaucratic (entrepreneurial) structures lack standardisation of tasks. This structure is most common in smaller organisations and is best used to solve simple tasks. The structure is totally centralised. The strategic leader makes all key decisions and most communication is done by one on one conversations. It is particularly useful for new (entrepreneurial) business as it enables the founder to control growth and development.

Bureaucratic Structures

Bureaucratic structures have a certain degree of standardisation. They are better suited for more complex or larger scale organisations. They usually adopt a tall structure. Then tension between bureaucratic structures and non-bureaucratic is echoed in Burns and Stalker distinction between mechanistic and organic structures.

Post-Bureaucratic

The term of post-bureaucratic is used in two senses in the organisational literature: one generic and one much more specific. In the generic sense the term post bureaucratic is often used to describe a range of ideas developed since the 1980s that specifically contrast themselves with Weber's ideal type Bureaucracy. This may include Total Quality Management, Culture Management and the Matrix Organisation amongst others. None of these however has left behind the core tenets of Bureaucracy. Hierarchies still exist, authority is still Weber's rational, legal type, and the organisation is still rule bound. Heckshcer, arguing along these lines, describes them as cleaned up bureaucracies, rather than a fundamental shift away from bureaucracy. Gideon Kunda, in his classic study of culture management at 'Tech' argued that 'the essence of bureaucratic control - the formalisation, codification and enforcement of rules and regulations - does not change in principle.....it shifts focus from organisational structure to the organisation's culture'.

Another smaller group of theorists have developed the theory of the Post-Bureaucratic Organisation provide a detailed discussion which attempts to describe an organisation that is fundamentally not bureaucratic. Charles Heckscher has developed an ideal type Post-Bureaucratic Organisation in which decisions are based on dialogue and consensus rather than authority and command, the organisation is a network rather than a hierarchy, open at the boundaries; there is an emphasis on meta-decision making rules rather than decision making rules. This sort of horizontal decision making by consensus model is often used in Housing cooperatives, other Cooperatives and when running a non-profit or Community organisation. It is used in order to encourage participation and help to empower people who normally experience Oppression in groups.

Still other theorists are developing a resurgence of interest in Complexity Theory and Organisations, and have focused on how simple structures can be used to engender organisational adaptations. For instance, Miner and colleagues studied how simple structures could be used to generate improvisational outcomes in product development. Their study makes links to simple structures and improviseal learning. Other scholars such as Jan Rivkin and Sigglekow, and Nelson Repenning revive an older interest in how structure and strategy relate in dynamic environments.

Functional Structures

The functional structure groups employees together based upon the functions of specific jobs within the organisation.

Matrix Structure

Matrix structure groups employees by both function and product. This structure can combine the best of both separate structures. A matrix organisation frequently uses teams of employees to accomplish work, in order to take advantage of the strengths, as well as make up for the weaknesses, of functional and decentralised forms. An example would be a company that produces two products, "product A" and "product B". Using the matrix structure, this company would organise functions within the company as follows: "product A" sales department, "product A" customer service department, "product A" accounting, "product B" sales department, "product B" customer service department, "product B" accounting department. Matrix structure is the most complex of the different organisational structures.

— *Weak/functional matrix:* A project manager with only limited authority is assigned to oversee the cross-functional aspects of the project. The functional managers maintain control over their resources and project areas.

— *Balanced/functional matrix:* A project manager is assigned to oversee the project. Power is shared equally between the project manager and the functional managers. It brings the best aspects of functional and projectised organisations. However, this is the most difficult system to maintain as the sharing power is delicate proposition.

— *Strong/project matrix:* A project manager is primarily responsible for the project. Functional managers provide technical expertise and assign resources as needed.

Among these matrixes, there is no best format; implementation success always depends on organisation's purpose and function.

Flat Structure

The flat structure is common in enterprenerial start-ups, university spin offs or small companies in general. As the company grow, however, it becomes more complex and hierarchical, which leads to an expanded structure, with more levels and departments.

Often, it would result in bureaucracy, the most prevalent structure in the past. It is still, however, relevant in former Soviet Republics and China, as well as in most governmental organisations all over the world. Shell Group used to represent the typical bureaucracy: top-heavy and hierarchical. It featured multiple levels of command and duplicate service companies existing in different regions. All this, made Shell apprehensive to market changes, leading to its incapacity to grow and develop further. The failure of this structure became the main reason for the company restructuring into a matrix.

Starbucks is one of the numerous large organisations that successfully developed the matrix structure supporting their focused strategy. Its design combines functional and product based divisions, with employees reporting to two heads. Creating a team spirit, the company empowers employees to make their own decisions and train them to develop both hard and soft skills. That makes Starbucks one of the best at customer service. Some experts also mention the multinational design, common in global companies, such as Procter & Gamble, Toyota and Hindustan Unilever. This structure can be seen as a complex form of the matrix, as it maintains coordination among products, functions and geographic areas.

In general, over the last decade, it has become increasingly clear that through the forces of globalisation, competition and more demanding customers, the structure of many companies has become flatter, less hierarchical, more fluid and even virtual.

Team Structure

One of the newest organisational structures developed in the 20th century is team. In small businesses, the team structure can define the entire organisation. Larger bureaucratic organisations can benefit from the flexibility of teams as well. Xerox, Motorola, and Daimler Chrysler are all among the companies that actively use teams to perform tasks.

Network Structure

Another modern structure is network. While business giants risk becoming too clumsy to proact, act and react efficiently, the new network organisations contract out any business function, that can be done better or more cheaply. In essence, managers in network structures spend most of their time coordinating and controlling external relations, usually by electronic means. H&M's is outsourcing its clothing to a network of 700 suppliers, more than two-thirds of which are based in low-cost Asian countries. Not owning any factories, H&M can be more flexible than many other retailers in lowering its costs, which aligns with its low-cost strategy.

Boundaryless Structure

The most radical concept in today's organisational design is the concept of 'boundarylessness', which seeks to overcome traditional boundaries between layers of management (vertical), functional areas (horizontal), as well as geographic boundaries. Some claim the boundaryless structure is a combination of team and network structures, with the addition of temporariness. Ikea, the world's largest furniture manufacture, has been successful in implementing the boundaryless structure. The company works closely with suppliers by providing technical assistance, leasing them equipment, and giving advice. It also refined the role of the customer, putting responsibility on them to cart the furniture home and assemble it themselves. As a result, the company can offer lower prices, which supports its low-cost focused strategy.

Virtual

A special form of boundaryless organisation is virtual. It works in a network of external alliances, using the Internet. This means while the core of the organisation can be small but still the company can operate globally be a market leader in its niche. According to Anderson, because of the unlimited shelf space of the Web, the cost of reaching niche goods is falling dramatically. Although none sell in huge numbers, there are so many niche products that collectively they make a significant profit, and that is what made highly innovative Amazon.com so successful.

As we can see, organisations develop, modify and change their structures so that they align with their strategies. And the main trend for the last decades seems to be coming back to flatter structures. Although this structure seems suitable for small companies only, large organisations can take elements of it in harder times. Being at risk of losing profits or even going bankrupt due to the major financial downturn today, a lot of companies are moving to flatter structures. Not only are they unable to maintain multiple management levels any more, they are also in need of a more flexible structure to cope with new threats.

PLANNING THE STRUCTURE OF YOUR RETAIL STORE

The organisational structure of a retail store will vary by the size and type of the business. Most tasks involved with operating a retail business will be the same.

However, small or independent retail stores may combine many sectors together under one division, while larger stores create various divisions for each particular function along with many layers of management.

For example, the small specialty shop may have all of its employees under one category called Store Operations. A large department store may have a complete staff consisting of a manager, assistant manager and sales associates for its Sporting Goods department, Home and Garden, Bed and Bath, and each additional department.

In order to define the store's organisation, start by specifying all tasks that need to be performed. Then divide those responsibilities among various individuals or channels. Group and classify each task into a job with a title and description. The final step is to develop an organisational chart.

The following is a brief outline of some of the divisions in a retail organisation.

Owner/CEO or President

Store Operations: Management, Cashier, Sales, Receiving, Loss Prevention

Marketing: Visual Displays, Public Relations, Promotions

Merchandising: Planning, Buying, Inventory Control

Human Relations: Personnel, Training

Finance: Accounting, Credit

Technology: Information Technology

As the store grows and the retail business evolves, the dynamics of the organisation's structure will change too. Therefore it is paramount to redesign the store's organisational chart to support the decision-making, collaboration and leadership capabilities that are essential during and after a growth period.

Size Building or Store You Need

What size building or store do you need? When planning your retail store, the amount of selling space will be one of the most important factors in selecting a location. It is can also be one of the most difficult to determine.

As with any new business, most of your assumptions will be based on industry research and comparing similar stores operating in similar locations. To get an estimate on how much selling space your store must have, divide the planned sales volume by your industry's sales per square foot.

Sales Volume ÷ Sales per Square Foot = Selling Space

Let's say you believe your proposed book store will do 10,000,000 per year in sales and market data says the average sales-per-square-foot in a book store is 6000. By plugging those numbers into our formula, the amount of selling space you will need is approximately 1666 square feet.

Besides selling space, remember to factor in extra square feet for an office area, stockroom, storage, and/or bathrooms. Although you may want room to grow, keep the size of the building close to your store's needs. A big store takes more inventory to fill and an empty looking store may not attract customers.

Store Design and Layout

Plan your store layout, atmosphere, and create irresistible visual merchandising displays. View floor plans and other retail store designs. Learn how to select and care for store fixtures, as well as using special lighting techniques to accent your products. Find store layout software and browse our resource of vendors selling store fixtures and displays

Ways to Turn Off Customers

As individuals, we all have our own little pet peeves. What may turn off one customer may not bother another. As retailers, we can't afford to turn off a single customer and image is everything. Keeping our stores neat and clean is not only easy to do; it is generally an inexpensive way to attract customers and create a pleasant store atmosphere.

Take a look around your retail store. Do any of the following situations exist? If not, look harder. Your store may be exhibiting some other offences you haven't noticed until now. Here are ten ways your store may be turning off customers:

Dirty Bathrooms

This customer pet peeve clearly deserves the number one spot on this list. Retail store restrooms should always be sparkling clean, whether they are open for public use or not. Make sure to stock the bathrooms with plenty of paper products, soap, trash receptacles and clean it daily.

Messy Dressing Rooms

Keeping the dressing room area free of discarded hangers, tags and empty packaging goes beyond creating a neat store appearance, it is also a good step towards loss prevention. Take a quick look for out of place items after each customer uses the dressing room.

Loud Music

Playing music in a retail store can help create a certain atmosphere for our shoppers. Music that is too loud, inappropriate or of poor quality can run a positive shopping experience.

Handwritten Signs

In this era of technology, there is no excuse for displaying handwritten signage. It is too simple to print a sign from our computers or use pre-printed signs. Printed signs simply look more professional and signs with hard-to-read handwriting can be a customer turn-off.

Stained Floor or Ceiling Tiles

It is true, accidents happen. However, our customers don't have to see them. Dirty carpet, stained flooring and ugly ceiling tiles can turn off many shoppers. Sweeping, vacuuming and mopping should be done on a regular basis. Consider hiring a professional cleaning crew to polish tile floors. Replace stained portions of carpet and ceiling tiles where possible.

Burned-out or Poor Lighting

Replace any burned out light bulbs as soon as possible. Make sure all customer areas of the store have ample lighting and take into consideration shoppers with aging or less than perfect eyesight. Your store should be well illuminated for all customers.

Offensive Odours

Customers understand if they visit a lawn and garden centre they will have to deal with the smell of fertiliser. The same goes for shoppers of a feed supply store. Certain odours are understandable and may even appeal to the customer's sense of smell. However, shoppers don't want to smell an employee's lunch drifting across the store. Use neutralisers to combat any offensive odours.

Crowded Aisles

Consumers like a selection but not if it means sacrificing

comfort while shopping. Be sure your store is designed to allow adequate space between aisles and keep walkways free of merchandise. Cramped spaces can ruin a shopping experience and turn off a customer.

Disorganised Checkout Counters

A stack of hangers, returned merchandise and sloppy work areas behind the checkout is a huge customer turn-off. This particular area where a customer's financial transaction is taking place should not show any signs of disorganisation. Like messy dressing rooms, a disorganised checkout counter can lead to theft. Keep those register areas neat and tidy.

Lack of Shopping Carts/Baskets

Your type of retail shop may not require a shopping cart or your store may be too small, but there's not a single type of retailer that wouldn't need at least some sort of shopping basket. If you hope for your customer to purchase more than one item in your store, be sure to have an adequate supply of shopping carts or baskets on hand.

How To Use Store Design to Reduce Shoplifting

It has been reported that employee theft and shoplifting combined account for the largest source of property crime committed annually. The easiest way for retailers to discourage theft in a store is by taking away opportunities to steal. A little thought into the store's layout and design can prevent theft before a loss occurs.

Difficulty: Average

Time Required: >1 Hour

Here's How:

1. *Checkout:* Design the store lay out so customers must pass the register area and staff to exit the

store. Never leave the register unlocked or unattended. Do not display merchandise near the store exits.

2. *Tidy up:* Keep the store neat and orderly. Full displays and straightened shelves allow employees to see at a glance if something is missing.
3. *View all:* Use mirrors to eliminate blind spots in corners that might hide shoplifters. Maintain adequate lighting in all areas of the store, keep fixtures and displays low for better visibility.
4. *Under lock and key:* Place small, expensive items in locked cabinets or behind the counter. Rest rooms and dressing areas should be watched at all times. Keep dressing rooms locked and limit the number of items taken in by each customer. Use alarms on unlocked exits and close or block off unused checkout aisles.
5. *Signage:* Signs and posters reinforcing security messages should be used. Post anti-shoplifting signs like 'Shoplifters Will Be Prosecuted' in clearly visible locations.
6. *Security:* Use security equipment such as closed circuit television, security tags and two-way mirrors. Uniformed security guards are also powerful visual deterrents to the shoplifter.

Types of Store Layouts

A well-planned retail store layout allows a retailer to maximise the sales for each square foot of the allocated selling space within the store.

Store layouts generally show the size and location of each department, any permanent structures, fixture locations and customer traffic patterns.

Each floor plan and store layout will depend on the type of products sold, the building location and how much the business can afford to put into the overall store design. Below are a few basic store layouts.

Straight Floor Plan

The straight floor plan is an excellent store layout for most any type of retail store. It makes use of the walls and fixtures to create small spaces within the retail store. The straight floor plan is one of the most economical store designs.

Diagonal Floor Plan

The diagonal floor plan is a good store layout for self-service types of retail stores. It offers excellent visibility for cashiers and customers. The diagonal floor plan invites movement and traffic flow to the retail store.

Angular Floor Plan

The angular floor plan is best used for high-end specialty stores. The curves and angles of fixtures and walls makes for a more expensive store design. However, the soft angles create better traffic flow throughout the retail store.

Geometric Floor Plan

The geometric floor plan is a suitable store design for clothing and apparel shops. It uses racks and fixtures to create an interesting and out-of-the-ordinary type of store design without a high cost.

Geometric Floor Plan

The geometric floor plan is a suitable store design for clothing and apparel shops. It uses racks and fixtures to create an interesting and out-of-the-ordinary type of store design without a high cost.

Store Fixtures and Displays

Learn which store fixtures, shelving, racks and other retail displays to use in your store. Tips for selecting gridwall, pegboard and slatwall. Find online resellers of retail store display, hangers, store-use items and more retail supplies.

Tips for Choosing Customer-Friendly Fixtures

Win customers by using retail display systems that are customer friendly: in other words, harness the powerful psychology of shopping. People love to shop. In fact, a great number of people consider shopping a relaxing leisure activity or even their hobby, with Business Network stating that 39 percent people in the United States "love to shop." So, retailers in general have an eager audience that is ready and willing to buy its products – but, they also have significant competition and so they must woo and win the attention of their potential customers.

One key way to attract and keep the attention of shoppers is to create an environment that is conducive to shopping – and one key way to do that is to use compelling, interchangeable store fixtures and retail display systems to keep your store fresh, interesting and appealing.

Here are several more important tips:

(1) *You can't use yesterday's store fixtures to capture the attention of today's shoppers.* An educational site in the United Kingdom – BizEd – published an article titled "The Psychology of Shopping." This article reported that retail giants of the 1970s relied heavily upon the philosophy of "pile it high, sell it cheap" and they found success with that philosophy. Since then, though, retailers are using increasingly sophisticated ways to capture the attention of shoppers – which means that you, as a retailer, also

need to use contemporary strategies, which include attractive retail fixtures, to keep customers satisfied.

(2) *Choose retail displays and fixtures that are uniquely suited to your target market.* Here's a great example of how not to structure your retail space. A blogger at a site for petite female shoppers was complaining that retailers – meaning those who cater to the petite – use retail displays that are not within comfortable reach of its customers. Now, does that make any sense? Of course not. Take a detailed look at your own store. In what ways are the store fixtures and retail displays that you're using not compatible with your customers' needs?

(3) *Design your space using retail display systems that make it easy for your customers to keep shopping.* The BizEd article also pointed out how successfully some retailers lay out their stores using retail displays that allow and even encourage a customer to keep browsing. Nothing blocks the customers from this path. So, again, take a look at your own store. What store fixtures or other items make it difficult for your customers to continue to navigate through all of your products? Remember, too, that an average person's field of vision tends to be around 170 degrees. Keep that in mind as you design your retail space.

Creating Attractive Displays

Creating an attractive product display can draw the customer in, promote a slow-moving item, announce a sale, or welcome a season. If your store front is fortunate enough to feature one or more windows, then you have one of the most proven (and least expensive) forms of advertising at your disposal.

Some stores located in a mall or other structure may lack windows, but don't despair. There are many places throughout the store to build beautiful displays. Take a look at the flow of traffic in your store. Are there any areas that are a focal point for customers? Your local community may have individuals or visual merchandising companies you can hire to dress your windows, but if you're concerned with saving money, the following tips will help you create an attractive display.

Visual Display Tool Box

Before designing a product display, put together a visual display tool box to keep on hand. By having all of these items in one location it will save time in actually preparing the display.

- — Scissors, Stapler, Two-Sided Tape, Pins
- — Hot glue sticks and glue gun
- — Monofilament Fishing Line
- — Tape Measure
- — Razor Blade/Utility Knife
- — Hammer, Nails, Screwdriver, Screws
- — Notepad, Pencil, Marker
- — Signage, Sign Holders
- — Glass Cleaner/Paper Towels
- — Props (Non-merchandise Items)

Take time to plan the display. Consider what you want to accomplish, develop a budget and determine a central theme. You may even want to sketch your display on paper. Gather your visual display tool box, the merchandise and any props. Make sure all materials and location (tables, windows, racks) are clean. Choose a slow time of the day or build the display after hours.

Elements of Effective Visual Merchandising

- — *Balance:* Asymmetrical rather than symmetrical balance with the display.

— *Size of objects:* Place the largest object into display first.
— *Colour:* Helps set mood and feelings.
— *Focal Point:* Where product and props/signage and background come together.
— *Lighting:* Should accent focal point, if possible.
— *Simplicity:* Less is more so know when to stop and don't add too many items.

Once the display is finished, add appropriate signage. Take photos of the display and keep record of the product sales during the display's existence. Save your information in a file folder for easy reference. By documenting its success, you can re-create the display next year or if it flops, you can make sure you don't repeat the same mistakes.

Like any other aspect of retailing, creating an attractive display takes a little skill and lots of trial and error. As your store changes, so will your opportunities for visual displays. Keep working at designing eye-catching and innovative ways to make your retail store profitable through visual merchandising.

STAFFING A RETAIL BUSINESS

As your business begins to grow and evolve, you'll be challenged by the decision to expand. If you are doing all of the work yourself, your first thought may be to hire employees. Before you begin the hiring process, take a moment to determine whether or not you really need the help.

Time Management

Are you doing everything you can to make your time as productive as possible in your store? Becoming better organised may eliminate the need for outside help. If you're having trouble managing your time, sign up for a seminar at your local library or college. Many retail owners try to wear all the hats and then feel they need to hire help. You can reduce some of the workload by outsourcing any part of your business that would be better served by a professional. Bookkeeping, marketing and information technology are areas that may be outsourced. Don't expect to have a lot of free time on your hands right away if you hire a new employee. Your new management role will involve a lot of time in the hiring process, the training of the new worker and the additional payroll paperwork. These new responsibilities will require you to have the organisational aspects under control.

Hiring is Expensive

Can you afford an employee? Hiring an employee is an investment but for each new hire your retail business makes, valuable resources like time, energy and money are dedicated to the effort. Examine your operating budget. Is there room to pay an extra worker? Keep in mind that you'll need to pay at least the minimum hourly wage and you'll also have payroll taxes and workers compensation to pay. An extra employee may generate enough new sales to more than compensate the salary of the employee. The additional help could give you a chance to produce more products or serve more customers efficiently. If the added business does not outweigh the minimum salary that you would have to pay, then consider other alternatives to hiring a permanent employee. There are many staffing options available and each has some pros and cons.

Staffing Options

Full-time employees: A person who works a set number of hours and generally receives benefits like health, dental and life insurance along with a standard salary is considered full-time. Having someone around full-time can provide a peace of mind knowing someone is minding the store even when you can't be there. There are also many labour laws which govern the full-time worker.

Part-time employees: These workers may offer more flexibility in scheduling and cost less than full-time employees, but you may spend extra time in training more people and if they have jobs elsewhere, worker loyalty may be compromised.

Temporary employees: Staffing agencies usually charge for the convenience of providing full service, as they handle the payroll administration and fringe benefits. However, temporary help may be usefull for the short-term projects such as the busy holiday selling season.

Independent contractors: Contractors usually provide work on a project-by-project basis where specialised training or certain skills are required. Fees for work performed are paid based on results and negotiated in advance. Be sure to have a written contract in place before hiring independent contractors.

Once your business becomes successful, you will obviously need help on a temporary or permanent basis. Good employees can be a business's biggest asset but the legal and accounting concerns that come with hiring can almost make it seem having employees is more trouble than it's worth. Be sure you understand all the responsibilities before recruiting and hiring.

Think for a moment how important staffing is to your retail store. To your customers, your staff represents a significant part of why they buy from your business. The type of interaction your staff has with your customers - whether good or bad — determines in large part whether your customers become frequent buyers and continue to patronise your business again and again.

Just as important, if you ever want to be able to "get away" from the business for a few days or longer, you need staff that is competent and well trained.

Hiring and retaining quality employees is not as easy as it used to be. Independent retailers need every advantage they can get in attracting and keeping those staff members that make their business run.

6

RETAIL MARKETING MIX

The Retail Mix is a marketing term that refers to the variables that a retailer can combine in alternative ways to arrive at a marketing strategy for attracting its consumers. The variables usually include factors such as: merchandise variety and assortment and services offered, pricing, advertising, promotion and layout, store design, store location, and visual merchandising.

Marketing your business is about how you position it to satisfy your market's needs. There are four critical elements in marketing your products and business. They are the four P's of marketing.

1. *Product.* The right product to satisfy the needs of your target customer.
2. *Price.* The right product offered at the right price.
3. *Place.* The right product at the right price available in the right place to be bought by customers.
4. *Promotion.* Informing potential customers of the availability of the product, its price and its place.

Each of the four P's is a variable you control in creating the marketing mix that will attract customers to your business. Your marketing mix should be something you pay careful attention to because the success of your business depends on it. As a business manager, you determine how to use these variables to achieve your profit potential. There are four P's of marketing and includes worksheets that will help you determine the most effective marketing mix for your business.

PRODUCT

"Product" refers to the goods and services you offer to your customers. Apart from the physical product itself, there are elements associated with your product that customers may be attracted to, such as the way it is packaged. Other product attributes include quality, features, options, services, warranties, and brand name. Thus, you might think of what you offer as a bundle of goods and services.

Your product's appearance, function, and support make up what the customer is actually buying. Successful managers pay close attention to the needs their product bundles address for customers. Your product bundle should meet the needs of a particular target market. For example, a luxury product should create just the right image for "customers who have everything," while many basic products must be positioned for priceconscious consumers. Other important aspects of product may include an appropriate product range, design, warranties, or a brand name.

Customer research is a key element in building an effective marketing mix. Your knowledge of your target market and your competitors will allow you to offer a product that will appeal to customers and avoid costly mistakes.

If you are considering starting a new business or adding a new product, then make sure the product bundle will fit your business's strengths and weaknesses, and that it will provide an acceptable risk/return trade-off. For instance, if your business is very good at timely response to customers, then timely service should be an important part of your product bundle.

Think long term about your venture by planning for the ways you can deepen and broaden your product bundle. For instance, you may be able to take advantage of opportunities to add value through processing, packaging, and customer service. Other future growth may allow you to offer your product to different customers. Start-up businesses are most successful when they concentrate their efforts on one product or one market, like a restaurant or a car service centre does. Later growth may occur in the same location or may be in different geographic regions.

A different type of growth would be a diversification of products, with your business offering related products. Offering a whole range of products is most successful if the raw materials, production processes, and distribution methods are similar, which means you do not have to acquire new suppliers, skills and equipment, and distribution methods.

PRICE

"Price" refers to how much you charge for your product or service. Determining your product's price can be tricky and even frightening. Many small business owners feel they must absolutely have the lowest price around. So they begin their business by creating an impression of bargain pricing. However, this may be a signal of low quality and not part of the image you want to portray. Your pricing approach should reflect the appropriate positioning of your product in the market and result in a price that covers your cost per item and includes a profit margin. The result should neither be greedy nor timid. The former will price you out of the market; pricing too low will make it impossible to grow.

As a manager, you can follow a number of alternative pricing strategies. In the next column are eight common pricing strategies. Some price decisions may involve complex calculation methods, while others are intuitive judgments. Your selection of a pricing strategy should be based on your product, customer demand, the competitive environment, and the other products you will offer.

- *Cost-plus:* Adds a standard percentage of profit above the cost of producing a product. Accurately assessing fixed and variable costs is an important part of this pricing method.
- *Value-based:* Based on the buyer's perception of value (rather than on your costs). The buyer's perception depends on all aspects of the product, including non-price factors such as quality, healthfulness, and prestige. Competitive: Based on prices charged by competing firms for competing products. This pricing structure is relatively simple to follow because you maintain your price relative to your competitors' prices. In some cases, you can directly observe your competitors' prices and respond to any price changes. In other cases, customers will select vendors based on bids submitted simultaneously. In those cases, gathering information will be more difficult.
- *Going-rate:* A price charged that is the common or going-rate in the marketplace. Going-rate pricing is common in markets where most firms have little or no control over the market price.
- *Skimming:* Involves the introduction of a product at a high price for affluent consumers. Later, the price is decreased as the market becomes saturated.
- *Discount:* Based on a reduction in the advertised price. A coupon is an example of a discounted price.

— *Loss-leader:* Based on selling at a price lower than the cost of production to attract customers to the store to buy other products.

— *Psychological:* Based on a price that looks better.

After you decide on your pricing strategy, the amount of money you will actually receive may be complicated by other pricing aspects that will decrease (or increase) the actual amount of money you receive. You will also have to decide how to determine:

— *Payment period:* Length of time before payment is received.

— *Allowance:* Price reductions given when a retailer agrees to undertake some promotional activity for you, such as maintaining an in-store display.

— *Seasonal allowances:* Reductions given when an order is placed during seasons that typically have low sales volumes to entice customers to buy during slow times.

— *Bundling of products/services:* Offering an array of products together.

— *Trade discounts (also called "functional discounts"):* Payments to distribution channel members for performing some function such as warehousing and shelf stocking.

— *Price flexibility:* Ability of salesperson or reseller to modify price.

— *Price differences among target customer groups:* Pricing variance among target markets.

— *Price differences among geographic areas:* Pricing variance among geographic regions.

— *Volume discounts and wholesale pricing:* Price reductions given for large purchases.

- *Cash and early payment discounts:* Policies to speed payment and thereby provide liquidity.
- *Credit terms:* Policies that allow customers to pay for products at a later date.

Your options will vary depending on how you choose to sell your product. For instance, if you make a product but don't sell it directly to the customer, then you will want to know who sets the retail price and what margin they will require. Tracing the path of your product from production to final purchase is a useful exercise to discover this information. The research needed to understand the pricing along the distribution path will be more than worth the time it takes.

Whatever your price may be, ultimately it must cover your costs, contribute to your image by communicating the perceived value of your product, counter the competition's offer, and avoid deadly price wars. Remember, price is the one "P" that generates revenue, while the other three "P's" incur costs. Effective pricing is important to the success of your business.

PLACE

"Place" refers to the distribution channels used to get your product to your customers. What your product is will greatly influence how you distribute it. If, for example, you own a small retail store or offer a service to your local community, then you are at the end of the distribution chain, and so you will be supplying directly to the customer. Businesses that create or assemble a product will have two options: selling directly to consumers or selling to a vendor.

Direct Sales

As a producer, you must decide if supplying direct is appropriate for your product, whether it be sales through retail, door-to-door, mail order, e-commerce, on-site, or some other method. An advantage of direct sales would be the contact you gain by meeting customers face to face. With this contact you can easily detect market changes that occur and adapt to them. You also have complete control over your product range, how it is sold, and at what price.

Direct sales may be a good place to start when the supply of your product is limited or seasonal. For example, direct sales for many home-produced products can occur through home-based sales, markets, and stands. However, direct sales require that you have an effective retail interface with your customers, which may be in person or electronic. If developing and maintaining this retail interface is not of interest to you or you are not good at it, you should consider selling through an intermediary.

RESELLER SALES

Instead of selling directly to the consumer, you may decide to sell through an intermediary such as a wholesaler or retailer who will resell your product. Doing this may provide you with a wider distribution than selling direct while decreasing the pressure of managing your own distribution system. Additionally, you may also reduce the storage space necessary for inventory. One of the most important reasons for selling through an intermediary is access to customers. In many situations, wholesalers and retailers have customer connections that would not be possible to obtain on your own. However, in selling to a reseller you may lose contact with your end consumer. In some cases, you may also lose some of your company identity. For example, your distributor may request that your product be sold under the reseller's brand name.

One factor that may influence whether you can find an intermediary to handle your product is production flow. Wholesalers want a steady year-round supply of product to distribute. If you can deliver a steady year-round supply that is of consistent quality, then selling through an intermediary may be a good strategy for you.

MARKET COVERAGE

No matter whether you sell your product direct or through a reseller, you must decide what your coverage will be in distributing your product. Will you pursue intensive, selective, or exclusive coverage?

Intensive distribution is widespread placement in as many places as possible, often at low prices. Large businesses often market on a nationwide level with this method. Convenience products—ones that consumers buy regularly and spend little time shopping for, like chewing gum—do better with intensive (widespread) distribution.

Selective distribution narrows distribution to a few businesses. Often, upscale products are sold through retailers that only sell high-quality products. With this option, it may be easier to establish relationships with customers. Products that people shop around for sell better with selective distribution.

Exclusive distribution restricts distribution to a single reseller. You may become the sole supplier to a reseller who, in turn, might sell only your product. You may be able to promote your product as prestigious with this method, though you might sacrifice sales volume. Specialty products tend to perform better with exclusive distribution.

PROMOTION

"Promotion" refers to the advertising and selling part of

marketing. It is how you let people know what you've got for sale. The purpose of promotion is to get people to understand what your product is, what they can use it for, and why they should want it. You want the customers who are looking for a product to know that your product satisfies their needs. To be effective, your promotional efforts should contain a clear message targeted to a specific audience reached via an appropriate channel. Your target audience will be the people who use or influence the purchase of your product. You should focus your market research efforts on identifying these individuals. Your message must be consistent with your overall marketing image, get your target audience's attention, and elicit the response you desire, whether it is to purchase your product or to form an opinion. The channel you select for your message will likely involve use of a few key marketing channels. Promotion may involve advertising, public relations, personal selling, and sales promotions. A key channel is advertising. Advertising methods to promote your product or service include the following:

- *Radio:* Radio advertisements are relatively inexpensive ways to inform potential local customers about your business. Mid-to-late week is generally the best time to run your radio ad.
- *Television:* Television allows access to regional or national audiences, but may be more expensive than other options.
- *Print:* Direct mail and printed materials, including newspapers, consumer and trade magazines, flyers, and a logo, allow you to explain what, when, where, and why people should buy from you. You can send letters, fact sheets, contests, coupons, and brochures directly to new or old customers on local, regional, or national levels.

- *Electronic:* Company Web sites provide useful information to interested consumers and clients. Password-protected areas allow users to more intimately interact with you. Advertisements allow broad promotion of your products. Direct e-mail contact is possible if you have collected detailed customer information.
- *Word of mouth:* Word of mouth depends on satisfied customers (or dissatisfied customers) telling their acquaintances about the effectiveness of your products.
- *Generic:* Generic promotion occurs when no specific brand of product is promoted, but rather a whole industry is advertised. For instance, generic advertising is commonly found for milk, Bread and Butter and eggs.

Public relations (PR) usually focuses on creating a favourable business image. Important components of a good public relations programme include being a good neighbour, being involved in the community, and providing open house days. News stories, often initiated through press releases, can be good sources of publicity.

Personal selling focuses on the role of a salesperson in your communication plans. Sales people can tailor communication to customers and are very important in building relationships. While personal selling is an important tool, it is costly. So you should make efforts to target personal selling carefully.

Sales promotions are special offerings designed to encourage purchases. Promotions might include free samples, coupons, contests, incentives, loyalty programmes, prizes, and rebates. Other programmes might focus on educating customers through seminars or reaching them through trade shows. Your target audience may be more receptive to one method than another.

7

RETAIL PRICING STRATEGIES

Setting the right price is a crucial step toward achieving that profit. Retailers are in business to make a profit, but figuring out what and how to price products may not come easily. Before we can determine which retail pricing strategy to use in setting the right price, we must know the costs associated with the products. Two key elements in factoring product cost is the cost of goods and the amount of operating expense.

The cost of goods includes the amount paid for the product, plus any shipping or handling expenses. The cost of operating the business, or operating expense, includes overhead, payroll, marketing and office supplies. Regardless of the pricing strategy used, the retail price of the products should more than cover the cost of obtaining the goods plus the expenses related to operating the business. A retailer simply cannot succeed in business if they continue to sell their products below cost.

The pricing strategy portion of the marketing plan involves determining how you will price your product or service; the price you charge has to be competitive but still allow you to make a reasonable profit.

The most common question small business people have about the pricing strategy section of the marketing plan is, "How do you know what price to charge?" Basically you set your pricing through a process of calculating your costs, estimating the benefits to consumers, and comparing your products, services, and prices to others that are similar.

Set your pricing by examining how much it cost you to produce the product or service and adding a fair price for the benefits that the customer will enjoy. Examining what others are charging for similar products or services will guide you when you're figuring out what a "fair" price for such benefits would be. You may find it useful to conduct a Breakeven Analysis.

The pricing strategy you outline in your marketing plan will answer the following questions:

What is the cost of your product or service? Make sure you include all your fixed and variable costs when you're calculating this; the cost of labour and materials are obvious, but you may also need to include freight costs, administrative costs, and/or selling costs, for example.

How does the pricing of your product or service compare to the market price of similar products or services?

Explain how the pricing of your product or service is competitive. For instance, if the price you plan to charge is lower, why are you able to do this? If it's higher, why would your customer be willing to pay more? This is where the "strategy" part of the pricing strategy comes into play; will your business be more competitive if you charge more, less, or the same as your competitors and why?

What kind of ROI (Return On Investment) are you expecting with this pricing strategy, and within what time frame?

RETAIL PRICING STRATEGIES

Retailers will also need to examine their channels of distribution and research what the market is willing to pay. Many pricing strategies exist and each is used based on particular a set of circumstances. Here are a few of the more popular pricing strategies to consider:

Mark-up Pricing

Markup on cost can be calculated by adding a pre-set (often industry standard) profit margin, or percentage, to the cost of the merchandise.

Markup on retail is determined by dividing the dollar markup by retail. Be sure to keep the initial mark-up high enough to cover price reductions, discounts, shrinkage and other anticipated expenses, and still achieve a satisfactory profit. Retailers with a varied product selection can use different mark-ups on each product line.

Vendor Pricing

Manufacturer retail price (MRP) is a common strategy used by the smaller retail shops to avoid price wars and still maintain a decent profit. Some suppliers have minimum advertised prices but also suggest the retail pricing. By pricing products with the suggested retail prices supplied by the vendor, the retailer is out of the decision-making process. Another issue with using pre-set prices is that it doesn't allow a retailer to have an advantage over the competition.

Competitive Pricing

Consumers have many choices and are generally willing to shop around to receive the best price. Retailers considering a competitive pricing strategy will need to provide outstanding customer service to stand above the competition.

Pricing below competition simply means pricing products lower than the competitor's price. This strategy works well if the retailer negotiates the best prices, reduces costs and develops a marketing strategy to focus on price specials.

Prestige pricing, or pricing above competition, may be considered when location, exclusivity or unique customer service can justify higher prices. Retailers that stock high-quality merchandise that isn't available at any other location may be quite successful in pricing their products above competitors.

Psychological Pricing

Psychological pricing is used when prices are set to a certain level where the consumer perceives the price to be fair. The most common method is odd-pricing using figures that end in 5, 7 or 9.

Other Pricing Strategies

Keystone pricing is not used as often as it once was. Doubling the cost paid for merchandise was once the rule of pricing products, but very few products these days allow a retailer to keystone the product price. Multiple pricing is a method which involves selling more than one product for one price. Not only is this strategy great for markdowns or sales events, but retailers have noticed consumers tend to purchase in larger amounts where the multiple pricing strategy is used.

Discount pricing and price reductions are a natural part of retailing. Discounting can include coupons, rebates, seasonal prices and other promotional markdowns. Merchandise priced below cost is referred to as loss leaders. Although retailers make no profit on these discounted items, the hope is consumers will purchase other products at higher margins during their visit to the store.

As you develop the best pricing model for your retail business, understand the ideal pricing strategy will depend on more than costs. It is difficult to say which component of pricing is more important than another. Just keep in mind, the right product price is the price the consumer is willing to pay, while providing a profit to the retailer.

CHOOSING PRODUCTS TO SELL

Choosing a product for your retail store to sell may very well be the most difficult decision you will need to make when starting a retail business. The choices are limitless and the task may be overwhelming at first. Not only should there be a demand for your products, but it must be profitable and something you enjoy selling. Before you commit to a product or product line, consider the following factors while deciding what products to sell.

Marketability

Let's face it, it won't matter what products you sell if your customers aren't buying. Before considering what product to sell, determine what market you want to sell to. Once you know what kind of customer you want, then you'll be able to determine their needs. If your products only appeal greatly to some people, it may not be enough to sustain a business. Your product selection doesn't have to appeal to all of the population but it should be something you can convince a large percentage of shoppers they need.

Profit Margin

Selling big ticket items is generally more profitable, but can require more credibility to sell. When you look at the price of the product, don't forget to calculate direct and indirect costs (like overhead) of selling your goods. You may find your profit isn't sufficient even though sales are good. The best selling products won't ever earn any real money if your margin is too small.

Consumable

Choose a product with recurring sales value. A consumable item that needs to be replaced on a regular basis is one way a retailer can establish long-term sales. By establishing a customer base with recurring products, customers will continue to come back to you to buy more as they use up the products. Additionally, satisfied customers are more open to recommendations for related products.

What's Popular

When it comes to selecting products to sell based on what's popular, timing is extremely important. New trends and products can be a great boost to your business but you'll need to be at the beginning of the product lifecycle in order to be successful. Learning to pick a hot product before it becomes hot is a valuable skill that comes from knowing your market.

Competition

Competition is healthy and there are ways other than volume and price a smaller store can compete with larger retailers. On the other hand, the more unique the product, the less chance of competition.

Private Label

One way to guarantee having a truly unique product line is to make the item yourself. Another way is to partner with a small business that makes a product you would enjoy selling. Also consider private label products which will allow you to brand an item made by another person.

Quality

Product quality is extremely important when your reputation is on the line.

Diversity

Keep your product offering simple in the beginning. If your product line is narrow and focused, then your marketing efforts can be just as tightly focused, which will bring you the best results for your marketing dollars. As your business grows, so can your product line as long as you keep new products compatible with the type of business, your location and your market.

Some questions to keep in mind while selecting products for resale.

- Would you buy it and use it yourself?
- Can you see yourself getting excited about this product or service?
- Would you sell it to someone you know?
- Is there a real need for the product in today's market?
- Can you imagine yourself selling this item for the next several?

The key to having a successful business is to know your products and to believe in the merchandise that you are selling. If you do not believe in the product yourself, then you probably won't be successful at selling it. Keep brainstorming and you'll find a product or product line that meets both the needs of your target market and your own ability to locate it, purchase it and resell it.

How much should you charge for your product or service

One of the most difficult, yet important, issues you must decide as an entrepreneur is how much to charge for your product or service. While there is no one single right way to determine your pricing strategy, fortunately there are some guidelines that will help you with your decision.

Before we get to the actual pricing models, here are some of the factors that you need to consider:

- *Positioning* — How are you positioning your product in the market? Is pricing going to be a key part of that positioning? If you're running a discount store, you're always going to be trying to keep your prices as low as possible. On the other hand, if you're positioning your product as an exclusive luxury product, a price that's too low may actually hurt your image. The pricing has to be consistent with the positioning. People really do hold strongly to the idea that you get what you pay for.
- *Demand curve* — How will your pricing affect demand? You're going to have to do some basic market research to find this out, even if it's informal. Get 10 people to answer a simple questionnaire, asking them, "Would you buy this product/service at X price? Y price? Z price?" For a larger venture, you'll want to do something more formal, of course — perhaps hire a market research firm. But even a sole practitioner can chart a basic curve that says that at X price, X′ percentage will buy, at Y price, Y′ will buy, and at Z price Z′ will buy.
- *Cost* — Calculate the fixed and variable costs associated with your product or service. How much is the "cost of goods", i.e., a cost associated with each item sold or service delivered, and how much is "fixed overhead", i.e., it doesn't change unless your company changes dramatically in size? Remember that your gross margin has to amply

cover your fixed overhead in order for you to turn a profit. Many entrepreneurs under-estimate this and it gets them into trouble.

— *Environmental factors*—Are there any legal or other constraints on pricing? For example, in some cities, towing fees from auto accidents are set at a fixed price by law. Or for doctors, insurance companies and Medicare will only reimburse a certain price. Also, what possible actions might your competitors take? Will too low a price from you trigger a price war? Find out what external factors may affect your pricing.

The next step is to determine your pricing objectives. What are you trying to accomplish with your pricing?

— *Short-term profit maximisation*—While this sounds great, it may not actually be the optimal approach for long-term profits. This approach is common in companies that are bootstrapping, as cash flow is the overriding consideration. It's also common among smaller companies hoping to attract venture funding by demonstrating profitability as soon as possible.

— *Short-term revenue maximisation*—This approach seeks to maximise long-term profits by increasing market share and lowering costs through economy of scale. For a well-funded company, or a newly public company, revenues are considered more important than profits in building investor confidence. Higher revenues at a slim profit, or even a loss, show that the company is building market share and will likely reach profitability. Amazon.com, for example, posted record-breaking revenues for several years before ever showing a profit, and its market capitalisation reflected the high investor confidence those revenues generated.

— *Maximise quantity*—There are a couple of possible reasons to choose the strategy. It may be to focus on reducing long-term costs by achieving economies of scale. This approach might be used by a company well-funded by its founders and other "close" investors. Or it may be to maximise market penetration — particularly appropriate when you expect to have a lot repeat customers. The plan may be to increase profits by reducing costs, or to upsell existing customers on higher-profit products down the road.

— *Maximise profit margin*—This strategy is most appropriate when the number of sales is either expected to be very low or sporadic and unpredictable. Examples include custom jewellery, art, hand-made automobiles and other luxury items.

— *Differentiation*—At one extreme, being the low-cost leader is a form of differentiation from the competition. At the other end, a high price signals high quality and/or a high level of service. Some people really do order lobster just because it's the most expensive thing on the menu.

— *Survival*—In certain situations, such as a price war, market decline or market saturation, you must temporarily set a price that will cover costs and allow you to continue operations.

There is no "one right way" to calculate your pricing. Once you've considered the various factors involved and determined your objectives for your pricing strategy, now you need some way to crunch the actual numbers. Here are four ways to calculate prices:

— *Cost-plus pricing*—Set the price at your production cost, including both cost of goods and fixed costs at your current volume, plus a certain profit margin.

So long as you have your costs calculated correctly and have accurately predicted your sales volume, you will always be operating at a profit.

- *Target return pricing*—Set your price to achieve a target return-on-investment (ROI).
- *Value-based pricing*—Price your product based on the value it creates for the customer. This is usually the most profitable form of pricing, if you can achieve it. The most extreme variation on this is "pay for performance" pricing for services, in which you charge on a variable scale according to the results you achieve.
- *Psychological pricing*—Ultimately, you must take into consideration the consumer's perception of your price, figuring things like:
  - *Positioning*—If you want to be the "low-cost leader", you must be priced lower than your competition. If you want to signal high quality, you should probably be priced higher than most of your competition.
  - *Popular price points*—There are certain "price points" (specific prices) at which people become much more willing to buy a certain type of product. Dropping your price to a popular price point might mean a lower margin, but more than enough increase in sales to offset it.
  - *Fair pricing*—Sometimes it simply doesn't matter what the value of the product is, even if you don't have any direct competition. There is simply a limit to what consumers perceive as "fair".

Now, how do you combine all of these calculations to come up with a price? Here are some basic guidelines:

- Your price must be enough higher than costs to cover reasonable variations in sales volume. If your sales forecast is inaccurate, how far off can you be and still be profitable? Ideally, you want to be able to be off by a factor of two or more and still be profitable.
- You have to make a living. Have you figured salary for yourself in your costs? If not, your profit has to be enough for you to live on and still have money to reinvest in the company.
- Your price should almost never be lower than your costs or higher than what most consumers consider "fair". This may seem obvious, but many entrepreneurs seem to miss this simple concept, either by miscalculating costs or by inadequate market research to determine fair pricing. Simply put, if people won't readily pay enough more than your cost to make you a fair profit, you need to reconsider your business model entirely. How can you cut your costs substantially? Or change your product positioning to justify higher pricing?

Pricing is a tricky business. You're certainly entitled to make a fair profit on your product, and even a substantial one if you create value for your customers. But remember, something is ultimately worth only what someone is willing to pay for it.

LOSS LEADERS

Loss leaders are goods or services offered at steep discounts (generally below cost) in order to attract new customers to a store. It is a time-honoured practice that has been met with much success, especially by large discount retailers. The intent of this pricing strategy is to not only have the customer buy the (loss leader) sale item, but other products that are not discounted.

When to use loss leader pricing:

— *Move overstock:* If you have inventory that isn't moving or if you're overstocked on a particular item, a loss leader can move it. By cutting the price of such an item, you'll not only free up the shelf space and reduce inventory, but you'll also increase cash flow.

— *Brand awareness:* If you would like to be known for having low prices then the loss leader pricing strategy will help associate your business with that belief. Keep in mind that people want good quality merchandise for less money and not junk.

— *Increased traffic:* Using loss leaders as a marketing tool can help gain new customers and increase return visits. People like a bargain and will likely come back to shop.

Loss Leader Precautions

There can be success in loss leader pricing, but be aware of some obstacles to the process. If done incorrectly, loss leaders can actually cause the business to lose money. Also, not all manufacturers and suppliers will allow their products to be priced under their minimum advertised price or less than what their other dealers are selling the same item. It is also limited or forbidden to sell products below cost in some states. In recent years, lawsuits have emerged (not all successful) claiming some loss leader pricing strategies are the equivalent to illegal business practices.

If you decide to use a loss leader, consider using loss leaders only when it's clear that the lost profit can be countered by the sales of other products or services. Avoid doing something illegal by making sure that there is a significant quantity of the sale item in stock and use 'while supplies last' in any and all advertisements.

Buying larger-than-normal quantities from suppliers may allow you a quantity discount, increasing the margin on the discounted price.

PRICE IS A PROMISE

Determine Your Promises

As you set your prices (or consider raising them), take stock of all the value factors that go into your price. What attributes of your product or service are noteworthy? Below are some examples of value factors that go into a product's or a service's price:

For a product

- — Quality of the raw materials
- — Finished product performance
- — Packaging
- — On-time delivery
- — After-sale service

For a service

- — Experience level of the service provider
- — Bottom-line impact of the final deliverable
- — Appearance of the service provider
- — Turnaround time on phone calls/emails
- — Ability to meet deadlines

As you can imagine, your ability to deliver various factors, over and above your competitors, directly impacts the prices you set...and get. If you promise certain factors, yet fall short on delivering them, your price will be challenged through customer complaints, delayed payments or customer defections.

8

RETAIL SUPPLY CHAIN

The retail supply chain spans the globe, and reaches deep into many diverse regions of the world. Potential energy, introduced into the retail supply chain through intelligent sourcing, strategic positioning, tactical postponement, logical processing and active management, increases business capacity and creates quantifiable economic value.

POTENTIAL ENERGY

Potential energy is measured in degree of ability to perform work, to displace some quantity of mass. A spring gains potential energy the farther it is pulled from zeropoint, up until it reaches its elastic limit. Pulling a spring past its elastic limit can nullify its ability to store energy. A straightened spring is, after all, no longer a spring at all.

These same forces exist within the supply chain, particularly within the extended global supply chain underpinning retail procurement. Here, too, stress is directly proportional to strain, and the further goods are offset from zero-point, the greater the business value that can be realised with reduced expenditures. This energizing is effected through careful coordination of location, timing, and mode.

Location

Since potential energy is created and maintained by position, certain locations produce greater than average power and efficiency. Drawing product from these areas of opportunity is analogous to leveraging a modern compound bow, rather than its historical counterpart. More elastic potential energy is created with less effort.

A retail goods sourcing example of such an area of opportunity is found in Southern China. The province of Guangdong has become the de facto manufacturing sector in southern China, initially due to its proximity to Hong Kong. This region produces commodities ranging from toys, to apparel, to footwear, to consumer electronics. In the past nearly all of these products were purchased in Hong Kong on a Free On-Board (FOB) basis. Goods ordered in full container loads (FCL) would be loaded at the factory, and drayed or moved by barge to the port of Kwai Chung in Hong Kong. Less than container loads (LCL) were most often transported to a designated Hong Kong consolidated freight station (CFS) and consolidated with other cargo to form full container load shipments.

There are a number of conditions affecting sourcing in this manner. The congestion encountered by shipments can be significant, affecting both customs clearance at border crossings and the capacity of CFS facilities. This is compounded during the peak-shipping season, a critical timeframe for North American retailers. It can result in transit delay and a loss of freight management.

Perhaps more importantly, retailers increasingly need much more than traditional cargo consolidation. Every link in the supply chain must provide more value to remain viable. Importers of retail goods increasingly rely upon value-creating services such seasonal pre-distribution programmes, inspection and quality assurance services, bar-code and label applications, pick and pack operations, stock and reorder replenishment, and other business-enhancing services. This can add a layer of complexity that adversely burdens the previous FOB shipment process.

Recently, several factors have intersected to create the potential for supply chain energy of position in southern China. An increasingly competitive global marketplace has forced merchandisers to negotiate per-unit costs down to minimal levels to support shrinking margins. Logistics expertise and infrastructure has emerged to enable importers to convert terms of sale from FOB Hong Kong to FOB China, allowing them to assume control of the international shipment process at an earlier stage, thereby avoiding many of the 'hidden costs' previously incurred.

Timing

Time is also a key factor in harnessing energy of position. The potential energy inherent in a raised golf club is wasted unless delivered in accord with a well-timed swing and follow-through. Timing is equally critical in the retail supply chain, and for similar reasons.

Reduced to common elements, all supply chains are amalgamations of goods, funds and information, both held and in motion. *When* these elements are set into motion is every bit as critical as *how* they are put into play. Lack of proper timing can result in swollen inventories at one extreme, and dire shortage at the other. Both push the supply chain past its elastic limit.

It is not coincidental that the oft-cited '4-R's' of retail logistics success includes timing. Perhaps more than any other industry retailing is dependent upon having the Right Product, at the Right Place, in the Right Condition, at the Right Time to satisfy a potential customers needs.

With the vast majority of retail sales meeting the classical marketing definition of an impulse buy, lack of discipline to any of these requirements will quickly lead to missed sales, and lost customers.

Understanding of, and focus on, supply chain timing can not only ensure that consumer demand is reliably met, it can increase efficiencies, and contain, and frequently reduce, costs. All conduits, be they physical pipelines, global supply chains, or retail sales channels, are bounded by their capacity. A store's shelves can only viably contain a set quantity of goods before the laws of diminishing returns and inventory depreciation constrain the ability to turn a profit. Pushing goods to the storefront out of synch with season, fashion, or demand incurs a significant opportunity cost, and does not drive sales.

For this reason retailers have increasingly sought out pull-based solutions, in which the capacities of both the supply chain and the selling space are brought into equilibrium, with demand providing the impetus for the movement of goods, information, and funds. The tools used to achieve the underlying supply chain transformation may include bypassing of traditional impediments and bottlenecks, time-definite distribution, and both direct to store and direct to consumer order fulfilment.

With an integrated multi-modal distribution network and cohesive supporting technology it becomes possible to consolidate packaged and labelled store-specific parcel shipments into economy producing full container loads at the port of origin, and enter them directly into the delivery network at the first possible port of discharge. This creates shipment efficiency, parcel level visibility, and retail capacity.

Mode

Mode is the third leg of the tripod that makes intelligent sourcing possible. Potential energy may be harnessed through a variety of mechanisms. The tool deployed is best selected by identifying the resource that creates the greatest possible benefit, while incurring the least possible opportunity cost.

The mode in which goods, information, and funds transit the extended retail supply chain should ideally be designated in exactly the same manner. The key, frequently overlooked, is to quantify the *total derived benefit,* weighed against the *aggregate* opportunity cost.

Focusing exclusively upon individual elements of a supply chain without regard for larger systemic ramifications can often result in unintended consequences. Initiatives undertaken to save money can have an inverse effect, which may go undetected initially.

The fact is that goods, information, and funds are fungible commodities, and quantities of one can always be exchanged for the other two. Whether this conversion is effected at a discount or a premium is directly impacted by the configuration of the supply chain through which they flow. Or fail to flow. It is important to note from the outset that there is no universal 'right answer.' The specific solution that creates the most supply chain value for a given retailer is a function of a range of factors, including store distribution, business model, and product and customer characteristics. The expertise required involves understanding of potential interactions.

Strategic Positioning

Where goods are drawn from, and when and how they are set in motion is only the beginning. How they are placed is equally critical. As noted earlier, potential energy is energy of position; the capacity to perform work increased by strategic situation. The nature of retailing, particularly on a national or international scale, creates the need for a multi-dimensional product positioning strategy. An effective strategy will entail multiple nested logistics considerations, including, but not limited to:

— Geographic channel distribution – where are sales effected?

— High opportunity demographic population distribution – where will retail business growth come from?

— Transportation conduit co-location – does it make more sense to be closer to the population centers, or closer to the means of reaching the population centers?

— Product pipeline – where does it make the most sense to take possession of goods?

Frequently, positioning is regarded as a stopping place, a point of suspended momentum in the supply chain. This need not be the case, unless the particular retail model employed most benefits from paused inertia. Alternatives include cross-dock and flow-through services, shared resources, and Just-in-Time solutions. Through strategic positioning it is possible to configure effective and efficient distribution as the path of least resistance.

Tactical Postponement

Potential energy is energy stored by virtue of position. If it is allowed to dissipate prematurely it cannot be leveraged. This principle has strong corollary in the retail supply chain.

Supply chain postponement does not imply a deliberate transit slowdown, though there are scenarios in which this can be productively utilised as a valuable alternative. Rather, it addresses the postponement of inventory, holding less of it in common pool in an unfinished state to avoid having to hold more of it in wider dispersal. Every discrete item a retailer sells represents a single stock-keeping unit (SKU).

Every variation, if sold uniquely, represents an additional SKU. Bring enough variety to the marketplace and a retailer may well increase sales, but they can easily increase held inventory as well. And, just as matter is energy, inventory is money. It is easy to overlook potential energy, which lacks the obvious force of its kinetic equivalent. This is also true in the retail supply chain, which is primarily seen as a conduit for moving goods, and not always fully recognised as a powerful medium for adding value to them as well. This is the essence of tactical postponement. Postponement strategies entail completing the production of a product to a state just short of its salable 'finished' condition. The level of completion is held at a branch point, from which the product can be quickly completed to form one of a number of consumer-facing SKUs. Completion typically requires easily effected configuration, kitting, or, at most, light assembly.

The end result is a pool of reduced inventory that can be quickly translated into one of many salable items in response to demand. The cost of excess inventory is contained, and variety is not sacrificed.

LOGICAL PROCESSING

Retail is an increasingly competitive sector of the global economy. Much of this competition is now coming from outside of traditional quarters. It takes the form of brand extensions from leaders in other segments, alternative channels reaching into the retail consumer base, and direct to consumer sales effected by producers and distributors. The convergence of competition in the retail market has made it imperative that retailers derive maximum utility from each and every resource.

The key is to define and execute logical supply chain processes, which increase holistic supply chain value as well as derive the most possible utility from individual elements, units, and commodities. Each transaction within a retail supply chain should ideally be accorded to the component that produces the greatest possible return value, while incurring the lowest possible opportunity cost.

All supply chains are defined by the interaction of goods, information, and funds. Inefficiencies in the deployment and utilisation of any one of these fundamentals will always result in penalties drawn against the other two. Conversely, an integrated solution choreographing the flow and interaction of these essentials will enable agile beneficial translation at parity or better. Consider the example of retail inventory rotation. With the amazing breadth, width, and scope of products sold today via the retail channel, it is not possible to define a single universal rotation strategy of mechanism that serves all needs. Some products are ideally suited to a first-in, first-out (FIFO) selection strategy. Other goods require the less arbitrary adherence to first-expiring, first-out rotation. Still others may require more custom strategies dictated by unique material identification sequences, product identifiers, and lot control considerations.

The common element is disciplined enforcement. It is not that the science of logistics is inherently difficult or arcane. Rather, like all true sciences, it is absolutely unforgiving of lack of process and attention to detail. Adherence to carefully refined process, conversely, unlocks a geometric progression of opportunities for cost containment and, frequently, reduction.

Rotation is a classic example of elastic potential energy in the retail supply chain. In all of the above rotation strategies, adherence to logistics discipline is the line of utility demarcation separating salable goods from disposal stock. Rotating out the goods with current viability, but the least remaining utility, enables the retailer to retain the goods with the greatest forward utility, to enable future sales. This is the equivalent to drawing a spring back to its elastic element for maximum power.

In many retail supply chains the greatest opportunities to increase resource utilisation are created by minimising and eliminating redundancies. This can be illustrated by considering an all too frequent cargo drayage phenomena. With a substantial proportion of goods sold in US retail stores originating in Asia, US West Coast ports are an essential gateway. Goods are typically discharged in full container loads onto intermodal double-stack train cars for drayage to an inland retail distribution center (DC). In many cases, this DC is *significantly* inland; it is not uncommon for these containers to cross the country under in-transit bond, to reach a DC.

Once there, the goods are broken out into store-level quantities for regional distribution. Ironically, this 'breaking out', expressed in French as retaillier, is the derivation of our word retail. Even more ironically, many of these deconsolidated goods are then sent back the way they came. In these cases, a sizeable percentage of the US population is often found *between* the West Coast ports of discharge and the inland retail distribution center. Whether they are reached en mass by local stores, or individually through catalogue or e-commerce sales, the end result is the same. Product must be shipped unnecessarily. Twice.

There are many avenues for improved utilisation in this example. They include cross-docking, optimised fulfillment, and even the aforementioned aggregation and pre-labelling of store-level shipments into full maritime container loads. Again, the solution deployed should ideally be the one that returns the most value, with the lowest opportunity cost and constraint on total resources. Crafting an extended global supply chain from logical processes produces an engine in which the utility of all component parts can be greatly expanded, harnessing business enhancing energy.

ACTIVE MANAGEMENT

With active management guiding the application of logistics expertise and infrastructure, the retail supply chain has the potential to be a key competitive advantage, an engine of business growth, and a producer of both customer and shareholder satisfaction. It can deliver far more than a consignment of consumer products.

It can deliver velocity, putting goods on store shelves and in the hands of customers at the most lucrative moment. It can deliver versatility, enabling a retailer to meet changing customer demands and demographics as opportunities, not challenges. It can deliver visibility, the insight essential to making informed retailing decisions. It can deliver value, which is, after all, the truest definition of retail success.

9

RETAIL FRANCHISING

Franchising refers to the methods of practicing and using another person's philosophy of business. The franchisor grants the independent operator the right to distribute its products, techniques, and trademarks for a percentage of gross monthly sales and a royalty fee. Various tangibles and intangibles such as national or international advertising, training, and other support services are commonly made available by the franchisor. Agreements typically last from five to thirty years, with premature cancellations or terminations of most contracts bearing serious consequences for franchisees.

A franchise agreement will usually specify the given territory the franchisee retains exclusive control over, as well as the extent to which the franchisee will be supported by the franchisor. The franchisor typically earns royalties on the gross sales of the franchisee. In such cases, franchisees must pay royalties whether or not they are realising profits from their franchised business.

Cancellations or terminations of franchise agreements before the completion of the contract have serious consequences for franchisees. Franchise agreement terms typically result in a loss of the sunk costs of the first-owner franchisees who build out the branded physical units and who lease the branded name, marks, and business plan from the franchisors if the franchise is cancelled or terminated for any reason before the expiration of the entire term of the contract.

Franchising dates back to at least the 1850s; Isaac Singer, who made improvements to an existing model of a sewing machine, wanted to increase the distribution of his sewing machines. His effort, though unsuccessful in the long run, was among the first franchising efforts in the United States. A later example of franchising was John S. Pemberton's successful franchising of Coca-Cola. Early American examples include the telegraph system, which was operated by various railroad companies but controlled by Western Union, and exclusive agreements between automobile manufacturers and operators of local dealerships. Earlier models of product franchising collected royalties or fees on a product basis and not on the gross sales of the business operations of the franchisees.

Modern franchising came to prominence with the rise of franchise-based food service establishments. This trend started before 1933 with quick service restaurants such as A&W Root Beer. In 1935, Howard Deering Johnson teamed up with Reginald Sprague to establish the first modern restaurant franchise. The idea was to let independent operators use the same name, food, supplies, logo and even building design in exchange for a fee.

The growth in franchises picked up steam in the 1930s when such chains as Howard Johnson's started franchising motels. The 1950s saw a boom of franchise chains in conjunction with the development of the U.S. interstate highway system. Fast food restaurants, diners and motel chains exploded. In regard to contemporary franchise chains, McDonalds is unarguably the most successful worldwide with more restaurant units than any other franchise network.

According to Franchising in the Economy, 1991-1993, a study done by the University of Louisville, franchising helped to lead America out of its economic downturn at the time. Franchising is a unique business model that has encouraged the growth of franchised chain formula units because the franchisors collect royalties on the gross sales of these units and not on the profits. Conversely, when good jobs are lost in the economy, franchising picks up because potential franchisees are looking to buy jobs and to earn profits from the purchase of franchise rights. The manager of the United States Small Business Administration's Franchise Registry concludes that franchising there is continuing to grow and that franchising is growing in the national economy.

METHODS OF FRANCHISING

The owner of the rights to the trademark is known as the Franchisor and the party wishing to use the trademark is the Franchisee. To operate as a franchise the Franchisee is obligated to pay fees and royalties in exchange for the rights to operate a business using the trademark provided by the Franchisor. The Franchisor is also required to provide support to the Franchisor such as training, supplying materials and equipment and offering business advice. There are two different methods of working with a franchise; Business Format Franchising and Product & TradeName Franchising.

Business Format Franchising

Business format franchising offers to most services and advice to the Franchisee. This is seen as a complete package for starting up a business, as the Franchisor will provide use of trademarks and images, business systems and help with location selection, layout, design and equipment, advertising and marketing, product supply and more. Staff training will also be provided along with continuing support. The franchise fee and royalties paid to the Franchisor go towards research and development of new products and systems that will be available to the entire organisation, including franchises. This style of franchising is popular in areas that involve unique products or services, such as food outlets and restaurants, salons etc.

Product & Trade Name Franchising

Product and trade name franchising offers a different type of franchise that has less involvement from the Franchisor. This style of Franchising includes the rights of the Franchisee to use trademarks and provide goods or services that only licensed locations may do. These include take away foods and drinks or specialised services. In return for this the Franchisor supplies the goods and equipment along with displays or vending machines. In this case the Franchisor may also help to secure locations for vending and advertisement.

BENEFITS OF FRANCHISING

Both the Franchisor and the Franchisee gain from the opportunities that are presented with franchises. For the Franchisor a franchise offers great marketing and brand awareness potential, as it introduces the brand to a new area without having to manage the location themselves. The organisation will also make a profit from any franchise that is operated on their behalf from royalty fees, initial franchise fees and the potential ongoing purchase of supplies. For the Franchisee, setting up a franchise of an existing business presents less risks than creating a new business. By having an established brand and help with many aspects of running a business, such as finance and marketing, from the Franchisor there is a greater chance of developing a successful business for both parties. Running a Franchise, like any business, does of course require dedication, business sense and drive and ambition.

ART OF FRANCHISING

Franchising is a business method, not a business form. The specifics of franchising lies in the franchise contract between franchisor and franchisee. Since the contract regulates many of the basic requirements on how the business is to be run, it is important that you carefully consider the terms of the contract.

The franchisee pays for the right to use the franchisors name and trademark and also for guidance on how to run the business in accordance with the franchisor's business concept. For the franchisee, franchising gives a possibility to use an already existing trademark and business concept. For the franchisor, franchising gives a possibility for expansion.

Plan the Start

A business run through franchising is still an independent company and you should plan the start as carefully as if you started the business all on your own, as an "independent" business. A franchisee also has to register the business at relevant public agencies and get information on, for example, book-keeping, taxes and insurance.

Business form for Franchising

It is common that requirements on the business form you need in order to run your business are included in the franchise contract. There is often a requirement that the business is run through a legal person. In this case it means either a limited company or a trading partnership.

Keep in mind the different requirements for the different business forms. It is essential in order for you to assess your possibilities to start up the business in accordance with the franchise contract.

For a franchisee it might also be interesting to compare income and costs as a franchisee and income and costs as an independent business. Among other things, it is important in order for you to assess if the business can reach the profit you want and if the terms of the contract are reasonable, considering your specific prerequisites.

Franchise Fees and Other Costs

As a franchisee, you pay for the right to use the franchisor's business concept. Usually you will pay a fixed amount when you start your business and then a monthly fee based on the sales for the given period. The monthly fees could cover, for example, the franchisors costs for service and joint marketing. Exactly how the franchise fee is calculated and paid, will vary from case to case. It is important to remember these fees when you make up your budget.

There are no standard types of contracts for franchising. Therefore it is important that you yourself carefully study the terms of the contract. That involves being aware of the rights and obligations that follow for you as a franchisee, before signing the contract.

DIFFERENT ASPECTS OF FRANCHISING

Franchising as a business method has different implications for franchisor and franchisee.

— For the franchisor it is a way of expanding and marketing his or her products or services, while the franchisee is sharing the costs for this.

— For the franchisee, franchising gives the possibility to start a business, using an already known and developed business concept. The franchisor has already carried the costs and risks involved with building up the business concept. This could mean that the franchisee will be able to get the business running faster than otherwise.

— The franchisee will also take part of the advantages a big company can offer, despite the own company usually being small. This can be true, for example, when it comes to purchase prices and marketing costs. The franchisee also gets access to the franchisors know-how and a network of other franchisees.

— As a franchisee you should be attentive to the terms of the franchise contract. To be a franchisee usually involves a limitation on your freedom of action when it comes to marketing, pricing and choice of suppliers. Go through the contract carefully, preferable together with a lawyer, before signing.

Franchise Contract

You should read through the franchise contract carefully. You need to know exactly what you are agreeing to in order to avoid unpleasant surprises and possible legal disputes.

TYPES OF FRANCHISING

The three types of franchising used are Product Distribution Franchising, Trade Name Franchising and Business Format Franchising.

Product Distribution Franchising

Product Distribution Franchising primarily involves a cooperation for the distribution of goods, a supplier or retail co-operation. Under what name or how the marketing of the goods takes place does not necessarily have to be regulated in the franchise contract. An example of this type of franchising is the brewery industry's sales of international soft drinks.

Trade Name Franchising

Trade Name Franchising means that the franchisee uses the trademark/business name of the franchisor in order to sell its own products or services. This type of franchising is found, for example, among international hotel chains.

Business Format Franchising

Business Format Franchising is a combination of the other two types of franchising and is found within various areas of business. The franchisee uses the franchisor's trademark/business name in order to distribute the franchisor's goods or services.

The franchise contract regulates, among other things, the freedom of action of the franchisee when it comes to marketing, running the business in general and choosing what goods or services to offer besides the franchisor's range.

Businesses for which Franchising Works Best

Businesses for which franchising is said to work best have the following characteristics:

- Businesses with a good track record of profitability.
- Businesses built around a unique or unusual concept.
- Businesses with broad geographic appeal.
- Businesses which are relatively easy to operate.

- Businesses which are relatively inexpensive to operate.
- Businesses which are easily duplicated.

ADVANTAGES OF FRANCHISING

Several years before, if one wanted to start his own business, his natural course of action would be to do it on his own, depending largely on his business instincts, limited know-how, and observation of the market.

The advent of franchising, however, brought a big change in business. Many have since become rich because of franchising. Franchising has indeed many advantages.

You Own the Business

A franchise is a duplicate of a successful business concept. The franchisee owns the outlet, therefore, he hires his own employees and oversees the management its day-to-day operations. He has high stakes in the business because his money is involved.

Ready Market

When one buys a franchise, he is buying an established concept that has a good record of accomplishment. The franchisee is allowed the use of the company's trademark and brand name. Because of this, the company is, in effect, giving the franchisee a license to market its products carrying a brand that is already familiar with the consumers.

Many popular franchises have instant brand-name recognition and have created a loyal following among consumers. Therefore, the franchisee is getting into a business that already has a ready market.

Continuous Support from the Franchisor

Although running his own business, the franchisee can tap the services of the parent company anytime he needs assistance. The services of the head office organisation are available to him, too, whenever he needs help. Furthermore, many companies have field operations personnel whom the franchisor can call on to help him deal with any problem he may encounter in the operation of the business. Most franchises being offered nowadays are turnkey operations.

Upon the signing of the franchise agreement and payment of the franchise fee, the franchisee receives the equipment and supplies required in running the business. Furthermore, the franchisor provides assistance in identifying a good business location for the new outlet.

The company assists the franchisee in negotiating his lease, preparing plans for outlet layout, shop fitting, and furnishing his store. It also provides assistance in determining the appropriate stock inventory for the opening of the business. This kind of support and the other benefits under the franchise agreement is what sets franchising apart.

Training

The franchisee is given the necessary training to start his business and eventually run it smoothly. The franchisee as well as his employees are taught all the business systems of the company covering product preparation, quality standards, business controls, recruitment of personnel, and marketing. A good franchisor will provide training to the franchise staff on a continuous basis.

Lower Capital Requirement

Compared to a non-franchise business, less capital is needed in a franchised business since the experience and tested system of operations of the parent company would already have eliminated the unnecessary expense incurred through trial and error.

Buying Supplies at Lower Costs

The franchisee is able to procure all necessary supplies at lower costs because the prices are negotiated by the company with the suppliers in behalf of all the franchise units. Because of the size and projected regularity of orders, the franchisor is able to get huge discounts.

Buying wholesale for the whole network means big savings for the individual franchises. This gives the franchises a big advantage over their competitors because they are able to reduce expenditures on a continuous basis. This procurement set-up is definitely more advantageous to the franchisee as against procuring supplies independently.

Extensive Promotional Campaigns

A franchise is the beneficiary of an extensive marketing campaign made possible by the sharing of the costs by the franchises. Many franchisees are required to shell out an advertisement royalty to the company as their share in the cost of promotional campaigns of the company, effectively spreading the cost among all the franchises.

This accounts for the large marketing resources of the franchisor enabling the company to avail of the services of top-calibre advertising agencies. Being situated in highly visible locations and benefiting from a huge promotions budget is a potent combination that is difficult for competitors to overcome.

Continuous Research and Development Programmes

The Company conducts continuous research and development programmes so that the business can improve the existing products and develop new ones to offer to the consumers. The marketplace changes rapidly and businesspersons have to keep up with the pace.

The chance to seize the opportunity of leading in the market is available for only a very short while. This stiff competition necessitates continuous research and development programmes for the company and the franchise network to succeed.

Acquiring the Status of the Company

As a franchise network expands, its stature in business becomes bigger. Mall owners prefer to have popular franchises in their malls because they want to present their shopping centres as a one-stop-shop where everything that customers want can be bought. Therefore, a franchisee will encounter very little difficulty in obtaining a lease in ideal locations.

Because a franchisee becomes part of the giant image of the parent company, he will probably find that running a franchised business is not only so much easier than being on your own, it can also be the best decision a franchisee has ever made.

Minimised Business Risks

Because the franchisee is buying a proven business concept, the business risks involved are largely minimised. The parent company has already resolved most, if not all, of the problem areas in its systems and procedures. What the franchisee is getting is a refined package of technical expertise, marketing strategies, and operational systems.

A Unified Set of Quality Standards

All franchise units are required to maintain a single set of quality standards insofar as product, customer care, and service are concerned. Here, the company will ensure that these standards are strictly adhered to and maintained in all its franchise units so that the whole network presents an image of providing quality products and services.

Benefits for the Franchisor

Franchising is a business concept that benefits the two parties involved. For the franchisor, franchising is advantageous because rapid growth can be more feasible even with minimum capital expenditures. When franchisees pay the franchisor for the chance to copy a proven business strategy, franchisors receive a steady flow of cash from royalties, which can be used to expand further.

Franchising a business can be like hitting two birds with the same stone: a franchise is being paid to expand it. Moreover, because others operate individual retail stores of the business that the franchisor originally established, direct managing responsibilities become the obligation of the franchisee. Hence, the franchisor will have more time in his hands to explore ways to further develop and promote the business.

The only way to develop as quickly is through franchising. Expansion is the only way a company can realise maximum profits. In franchising, there are not many obstacles to stunt the expansion of a company, therefore, there is a big possibility of really expanding the franchise network not only in the country but also even overseas. At present, franchising is the only business concept that can make that possible.

Franchised businesses grow rapidly, sometimes having several outlets in a certain area, pushing the competition out. All these benefits for the franchisor are, in turn, advantageous to the franchisees since the franchises are largely dependent on the success and stature of the parent company.

No other business concept can offer such an attractive and beneficial arrangement.

There are many advantages to be found in buying a franchise that make starting your own business that little bit easier. When faced with starting your own business it can sometimes be the simple solution.

DISADVANTAGES OF FRANCHISING

Although many people enjoy the benefits of franchising, there are still several disadvantages that a prospective franchisee needs to be aware of.

Buying into big and popular franchises is expensive. Their track record does not need much investigation since their outlets are most probably in every major town and city in the country, perhaps even abroad. Their popularity with consumers speaks well of the profitability of the brand.

However, a prospect eyeing such franchises must be ready with a large amount of money or be able to make the necessary financial arrangements since the franchising fee alone can command a hefty price.

On top of the original franchise fee, royalties and a percentage of business revenue of the franchise must be paid to the franchisor every month. In addition, the franchisor may also charge fees for the cost of advertising and promotional materials. These will be stipulated in the franchise agreement.

On the other hand, buying a little-known and perhaps inexpensive franchise can be attractive especially to those who would like to start their own business but do not have the kind of money needed to buy a popular one. Prospects need to be aware, however, that just because a business is offering franchises is no assurance that its franchises will be successful.

In some cases, franchising itself is the business of the company. In this case, the franchisor is only interested in selling as many franchises as possible regardless of whether the individual franchises will be successful or not. However, this is not to say that little-known inexpensive franchises are not worth looking into. Some of these may even prove to be a sound business concept that has just started.

Therefore, all franchises, whether popular or little known, must be investigated carefully before making a final decision.

In franchising, although the franchisee owns the business, he is not an independent entrepreneur. He must follow all of the instructions of the franchisor, sometimes down to the smallest details, to ensure uniformity with all other franchises. Franchising does not allow the franchisee much control over his business because he has to adhere to an agreed method of operation. A tightly written franchise agreement gives the franchisee little latitude to deviate from the system of the franchisor.

Some people may not be able to live with this arrangement for extended periods because the restraints being imposed by the franchisor may be too limiting for their own personal style. This is the reason why it is important for a prospect to match his intended business with his personality, preferences, and style.

There is always the possibility that conflicts between the own outlets of the franchisor and those owned by franchisees may occur, particularly if they are servicing the same general area. One may cut into the customer base of the other and franchisor and franchisee will ultimately be competing against each other to some extent.

It is also possible that there are too many franchises of the same brand in one area that franchises are pitted against each other. This scenario happens when the franchisor did not give much consideration to market studies but only to the financial gain with many franchises.

Factors such as interest rates, willingness of banks to extend loans to franchises, the condition of the national economy, and competition come into play once a business starts to operate. The franchisee must be financially ready to absorb the negative impact of these factors.

An inevitable aspect of franchising is the conflict that may arise between the franchisee and franchisor once the former starts losing money. More often than not, the conflict results in litigation, something that will be costly to both parties in terms of both time and money.

Tremendous efforts and resources on the part of the franchisor are needed to ensure the success of all its franchises. The bad news is that not all franchisors have access to such big resources, hence limiting their efforts largely.

Not all franchisors offer the same degree of assistance in starting a business and later on running it successfully. Some provide training just for start-up operations and the franchisee is left on his own after that. Others make assurances of continuous personnel training and support that they do not follow through on.

Deciding to get a franchise is good. However, its potential negative aspects must still be considered and addressed, because to be forewarned is to be forearmed. No franchisor is perfect, so it is up to the aspiring franchisee to objectively assess the profile of the target franchisor, and prepare for all the possible scenarios that might happen in the future.

Franchising can seem like the quick route to success, however if you are to succeed in business you need to know all the facts, otherwise you may well be wasting your time and hard earned money.

DETERMINING A GOOD FRANCHISE

Deciding to get a franchise is only the first of several major decisions a prospective franchisee will have to make. The next is determining the best franchise opportunity.

The best franchise opportunity is a totality of many factors. These factors are like parts that make up a whole. They work together to achieve a beneficial result. Foremost of these factors is the prospect's financial capability or ready access to financing since a large amount of money is required for the franchise fee, down payment on the lease, and other expenses. In addition to being financially ready, he should make a complete self-examination to determine his personality and preferences so that he can find the right kind of business that will match his style.

Preferably, the prospect must have conducted his own research and market study before setting up a meeting with the franchisor. This will enable him to inquire intelligently about important details relative to the company and the arrangements under the franchise. This way, he does not enter into something that he does not know much about, wherein he will have to depend mainly on the franchisor for information. This kind of information is unreliable since it has already been edited to come up with a highly convincing franchise presentation.

In asking questions, the prospect must solicit important information such as those about the track record of the company insofar as its franchises are concerned; how committed it is in providing continuous support to the franchise and ensuring its success; how effective its training and marketing programs are; and if the company has an continuing product research and development program to make the business updated and competitive. The franchisor must be able to provide this information to the prospect's satisfaction.

If the business is large and enormously popular in the market, its franchise network is most probably successful. Accordingly, the franchise fee alone will cost the prospect a large sum of money. If he does not possess the financial capability required by large companies, the next best thing is to look for a lesser-known company that has a high market potential but a lower franchise fee. However, the risks involved here are definitely higher than with a large-company franchise.

In considering the franchise offer of a less popular franchisor, the prospect has to conduct a thorough study on the background of the company, its present management, and the market potential of its products or services in his intended business location. He must also be able to find substantiated answers to the following questions:

- Is the business concept innovative enough to attract customers?
- Will it draw enough interest in the marketplace to make loyal customers?
- Is the company willing to allot a reasonable budget to fund marketing programs in the area to help the franchisee realise more profits?
- Am I willing to risk my money on a novel concept such as this?

— If so, am I up to the challenge of turning the franchise into a profitable venture?

— If the answer to all these questions is "yes," the other equally important factors must also be considered

The planned business site for the franchise unit is another crucial factor if the business is to succeed. Ideally, the business must be established in a place where there is a lot of human traffic, possibly inside a shopping centre, near a school, or downtown where all the shops are situated. It must also be easily accessible to its target market. In this regard, the franchisor's willingness to provide support in pinpointing determining the ideal location and negotiating the lease will be a good indication of his sincerity.

In addition, the prospect has to determine the availability of competent people in the area who can be considered for possible employment in his franchise. Staffing the business with quality employees who can be trained in operations and management will be an essential factor in running the business smoothly.

As the prospective chief operations officer of a franchise unit, the prospect must be assured of an effective training programme that will arm him with adequate knowledge in starting the business and running it smoothly later on. A good training programme for the employees should also be in place.

Furthermore, local legislations that are favourable to business will make the franchise opportunity more encouraging, assuming, that is, that the general economic condition is good for business.

The best franchise opportunity materialises when the prospective franchisee is financially ready; he has made a thorough study of his chosen company, its viability, products, and franchise network; he is assured of the commitment of the company to provide him continuous support; he has a good business site in mind; and the prevailing economic condition is conducive to starting a business.

The moment this opportunity presents itself, seize it!

FRANCHISE OPPORTUNITIES

Franchise opportunities are on the up and every day as awareness of the market grows and more people choose to opt out of the traditional 9-5 work routine and work for themselves. Due to this expansion, there is now a broad range of business franchises for sale becoming available on the market and profitable opportunities with realistic and provable income opportunities are in high demand as eager potential business owner look for the right Franchise opportunity.

Investing in your own franchise is a daunting decision with challenges to face, both physically and emotionally, with franchise opportunities the work load and level of responsibility are high and commitment has to be 100%, however previous experience isn't always necessary as there is a lot of guidance and help on offer.

When deciding on a business franchise, select the type of opportunity that best fits your interests, skills and financial needs and make sure you look at the franchise information available and make sure you resist buying a franchise until you have explored it fully.

Available Franchise Opportunities

There are different types of franchise opportunities available that can be found in franchise directory; Job Franchises are hands on businesses; Sales and Distribution Franchises involve selling and distributing products in your area; Executive Franchises operate a one-man, professional business; Retail Franchises requires investing in commercial property, staff and inventory to run a shop unit; Investment Franchises requires capital and a manager to run the business and, lastly, a Management Franchise entails the franchisee to manage a team of workers.

Franchise Opportunities Training and Support

Good franchisors will provide all the training, preparation and marketing you need. It is in their interests to help you out as much as they can as a successful business for you will benefit them too. You will pay a regular fee for this management service so make the most of their valuable experience and knowledge. Assistance will begin from the basics, help in putting together the business plan, selecting appropriate location and site, marketing techniques, and carry on through to negotiating funding packages with lenders.

Telephone support will always be accessible. If your franchise opportunity is IT based or in a specialist area then trained staff, technical support and expert advisors will be available to deal with your questions.

Business franchise opportunities do not guarantee success but franchisors understand that the more help and sound, practical advice and training provided in the first few months are critical to the success of the business and realise that as time goes by their help and guidance can be withdrawn slowly, replaced by a more general support programme, as the franchisee become adept in their business.

Whether you have to be involved with creating sales and the marketing of your service or product will depend on the kind of franchise you are buying into and the position you have within it.

In some areas franchisees will be required to generate business and people with some knowledge or experience in sales and marketing will have an advantage; however in others, such as job franchises, the franchisor takes responsibility for securing accounts leaving the franchisee to focus on providing a quality service.

Also, some management franchise opportunities take some responsibility for these areas thus allowing their franchisees to apply their time to building the infrastructure of the business.

CHOOSING A FRANCHISE

Choosing the perfect franchise yourself requires a great deal of though as there are many different aspects to consider.

Your Skills and Interests

This is the most important aspect when matching any kind of business with a person. By identifying your key skills you can discover the industry or role that is best suited to you. A reason for many people to break away from the standard 9-5 job is to do something that they enjoy, and by choosing a franchise in an industry that requires your skills and interests you will be working in an environment that you enjoy. A franchise is a commitment for several years, so it is best to choose a field that has long term appeal.

The most important requirement for any franchise is that you must be willing to work hard and put 100% into the running of your franchise as with any business. Success is never easy in any industry and by putting everything into the setting up and running of your franchise you will be giving it your best start. Good business sense is a requirement for running a franchise, and skills in this area will be invaluable to you and the business. Great organisation is also essential, as is time keeping and planning.

It is also important to note what kind of hours and times that you wish to work. Many areas, including Retail Franchises and Food Franchises require long and irregular hours, and if this would cause problems it is best not to chose these types of franchises. There are more flexible franchises that allow for working from home and with flexible hours in other franchises such as Childrens Franchises, Education & Training Franchises and franchises in Health & Beauty. These can often be fitted into a family life and can provide great opportunities.

Opportunity in the Market

It is best to choose a franchise in a market that isn't already saturated in your area with many other competitors. If there are competitors you need to see what advantage your franchise would have over them, such as price, better service or superior quality. It is also best to choose a franchise in a growing market so that your business can grow in turn. Knowing your local market is essential, and if there area has a need for the services that you can offer then there is great potential in the area for your franchise to succeed.

Costs

Finance plays a big part in choosing a franchise for yourself, as all of them require a level of financial commitment. Most franchises require an initial franchise fee that gives the franchisor the rights to operate under a trademark and brand, and then pay continuing royalty fees that pay towards continual development of the brand, the services and products that they provide. The royalty fee is also often used for ongoing training of the franchisee and their staff. There may be other fees associated with a franchise, such as advertising along with the requirement to purchase specialised equipment and all of your supplies from the franchisor. Before selecting a franchise it is best to have all of the possible information, including every detail about fees, and finances associated with running a franchise. This include ongoing costs, projected sales, costs and profits and can be quite accurate due to the experience of the franchisor with previous franchises.

10

RETAIL MERCHANDISING

Merchandising refers to the methods, practices and operations conducted to promote and sustain certain categories of commercial activity. The term is understood to have different specific meanings depending on the context. Merchandise is sale goods at a store.

Merchandising traces its growth to the rise of organised retail in the world. Initially as the retailers operated one or two stores, the function of buying the merchandise, pricing it, etc was much simpler. In many cases the retailer himself did it. However, when retailers started adding stores and categories, the work load on the buyers increased significantly. Often buyers had little information or time and they ended up using approximations based on sales volumes to allocate merchandise between stores.

LICENSING

In marketing, one of the definitions of merchandising is the practice in which the brand or image from one product or service is used to sell another. Trademarked brand names, logos, or character images are licensed to manufacturers of products such as toys or clothing, which then make items in or emblazoned with the image of the license, hoping they'll sell better than the same item with no such image.

Children

Merchandising for children is most prominently seen in connection with films, usually those in current release and with television shows oriented towards children. Merchandising, especially in connection with child-oriented films and TV shows, often consists of toys made in the likeness of the show's characters or items which they use. However, sometimes it can be the other way around, with the show written to include the toys, as advertising for the merchandise. The first major example of this was the TV show "He-man and the Masters of the Universe," in the early 1980s, but this practice has been common in children's broadcasting ever since.

Sometimes merchandising from a television show can grow far beyond the original show, even lasting decades after the show has largely disappeared from popularity. In other cases, large amounts of merchandise can be generated from a pitifully small amount of source material.

Adults

The most common adult-oriented merchandising is that related to professional sports teams (and their players). A smaller niche in merchandising is the marketing of more adult-oriented products in connection with similarly adult-oriented films and TV shows. This is common especially with the science fiction and horror genres. Occasionally shows which were intended more for children find a following among adults, and you can see a bit of a crossover, with products from that show oriented towards both adults and children. Sometimes a brand of non-media products can achieve enough recognition and respect that simply putting its name or images on a completely unrelated item can sell that item.

Promotional Merchandising

Merchandising, as commonly used in marketing, means maximising merchandise sales using product design, selection, packaging, pricing, and display that stimulates consumers to spend more. This includes disciplines in pricing and discounting, physical presentation of products and displays, and the decisions about which products should be presented to which customers at what time.

This annual cycle of merchandising differs between countries and even within them, particularly relating to cultural customs like holidays, and seasonal issues like climate and local sporting and recreation.

Trading Industry

In Eastern Europe, particularly in Russia, the term "merchandising" is commonly used within the trading industry and denotes all marketing and sales stimulation activities around PoS (point of sale): design, creation, promotion, care and training of the sales staff. Basically merchandiser is the one who is continuously involve in business promotion by buying and selling of goods.

Retail supply chain

In the supply chain, merchandising is the practice of making products in retail outlets available to consumers, primarily by stocking shelves and displays. While this used to be done exclusively by the stores' employees, many retailers have found substantial savings in requiring it to be done by the manufacturer, vendor, or wholesaler that provides the products to the retail store. In the United Kingdom there are a number of organisations that supply merchandising services to support retail outlets with general stock replenishment and merchandising support in new stores. By doing this, retail stores have been able to substantially reduce the number of employees needed to run the store. While stocking shelves and building displays is often done when the product is delivered, it is increasingly a separate activity from delivering the product. In grocery stores, for example, almost all products delivered directly to the store from a manufacturer or wholesaler will be stocked by the manufacturer's/wholesaler's employee who is a full time merchandiser. Product categories where this is common are Beverage, packaged baked goods, magazines and books, and health and beauty products. For major food manufacturers in the beverage and baked goods industries, their merchandisers are often the single largest employee group within the company. For nationwide branded goods manufacturers such as The Coca-Cola Company and PepsiCo, their respective merchandiser work forces number in the thousands.

AUCTIONS IN RETAIL STORE

Many retailers are using eBay but few small businesses are capitalising on live auctions. If you sell antiques or collectibles, chances are you know auction houses can be a gold mine of bargains for items to resell in your shop. Other retailers may not be aware of the deals they can find at an auction house. Local auctions are great places to purchase store fixtures, display props, merchandise and other items to be used in a retail store.

Store Fixtures

Watch your local paper for liquidation auctions of similar shops going out of business. A store permanently closing its doors may commission an auctioneer to sell out the entire inventory and fixtures to the highest bidders.

Round racks, 4-ways, grid wall, mannequins and other store fixtures can be purchased for just pennies on the dollar.

Don't limit yourself to standard chrome and glass store fixtures. Use your imagination. Wooden end tables, coffee tables, Hoosier cabinets and other vintage furniture make excellent display fixtures. An old armoire filled with new merchandise can serve as a centerpiece in your store. Corner racks allow a retailer to utilise space otherwise overlooked. A wooden ladder also works well to display hanging clothing.

Display Props

The cost of props can really add up if purchased new for each seasonal event. Look for holiday decorations auctioned by the boxed lots for very little money. Baskets, boxes, bottles, glassware, and pottery are all great props for creative visual displays that can be found at auctions.

Vintage items serving as display props can bring character to your retail shop. A child's sled or snowshoes can create a focal point among winter merchandise displays. An antique typewriter adds flair to office supplies, while a watering can or gardening gloves look great in a floral display.

Store Use Items

Before purchasing an item new, check local auctions for good used items. Cash registers, coolers, neon signs, small appliances, and lawn care equipment can all usually be found at live auctions well below retail price.

Merchandise

If your store sells one-of-a-kind items, auctions are great places to find unique merchandise. Auctions featuring estate sales or consignments can net savvy shoppers a fair price on goods for resale.

Before Attending an Auction

Understand auction terms: Educate yourself on commonly used auction terms such as buyer's premium, reserve and other auction lingo.

Preview items: Show up at least an hour early to preview the items up for sale. This is your time to look them over inside and out. Auction items are sold as-is so it is recommended you carefully examine any item you may be interested in purchasing. Photos from a flyer or pictures posted online may not disclose cracks, chips or the working order of an item.

Payment: Verify types of payment accepted. Many established auctioneers will take cash, good checks and credit cards. Some only accept cash. If you plan to resell the items you purchase at the auction, bring a copy of your resale certificate to register with the auctioneer or sales tax may be charged on your purchase.

Transportation: Bring an appropriate vehicle to haul your deals back home. The auction house may have a scheduled pick up time/day so be sure to ask if you unexpectedly purchase a large piece that won't fit in to the back of your car.

Like any buying trip, go to a live auction with a plan and a budget. Keep track of each item you buy and its final price. Buyers caught up in a bidding frenzy may later regret bad purchases. Once you've arranged your auction bargains in your shop, don't be surprised if customers ask to buy unique props and fixtures. Some retailers will put price tags on displays for that very reason. After all, retail is all about making money, isn't it?

CREATING ATTRACTIVE DISPLAYS

Creating an attractive product display can draw the

customer in, promote a slow-moving item, announce a sale, or welcome a season. If your store front is fortunate enough to feature one or more windows, then you have one of the most proven (and least expensive) forms of advertising at your disposal.

Some stores located in a mall or other structure may lack windows, but don't despair. There are many places throughout the store to build beautiful displays. Take a look at the flow of traffic in your store. Are there any areas that are a focal point for customers?

Your local community may have individuals or visual merchandising companies you can hire to dress your windows, but if you're concerned with saving money, the following tips will help you create an attractive display.

Visual Display Tool Box

Before designing a product display, put together a visual display tool box to keep on hand. By having all of these items in one location it will save time in actually preparing the display.

- — Scissors, Stapler, Two-Sided Tape, Pins
- — Hot glue sticks and glue gun
- — Monofilament Fishing Line
- — Tape Measure
- — Razor Blade/Utility Knife
- — Hammer, Nails, Screwdriver, Screws
- — Notepad, Pencil, Marker
- — Signage, Sign Holders
- — Glass Cleaner/Paper Towels
- — Props (Non-merchandise Items)

Take time to plan the display. Consider what you want to accomplish, develop a budget and determine a central theme. You may even want to sketch your display on paper. Gather your visual display tool box, the merchandise and any props. Make sure all materials and location (tables, windows, racks) are clean. Choose a slow time of the day or build the display after hours.

ELEMENTS OF EFFECTIVE VISUAL MERCHANDISING

— *Balance:* Asymmetrical rather than symmetrical balance with the display.

— *Size of objects:* Place the largest object into display first.

— *Colour:* Helps set mood and feelings.

— *Focal point:* Where product and props/signage and background come together.

— *Lighting:* Should accent focal point, if possible.

— *Simplicity:* Less is more so know when to stop and don't add too many items.

Once the display is finished, add appropriate signage. Take photos of the display and keep record of the product sales during the display's existence. Save your information in a file folder for easy reference. By documenting its success, you can re-create the display next year or if it flops, you can make sure you don't repeat the same mistakes.

Like any other aspect of retailing, creating an attractive display takes a little skill and lots of trial and error. As your store changes, so will your opportunities for visual displays. Keep working at designing eye-catching and innovative ways to make your retail store profitable through visual merchandising.

DIGITAL SIGNAGE IN RETAIL

Digital signage refers to a variety of technologies used to

replace traditional retail signs. Instead of static print signs and billboards, digital signage is composed of electronic signs dispersing content and messages in the most targeted, interactive way.

Liquid crystal displays, plasma display panels and scrolling message boards are a few of the more common in-store devices used to project full-motion video, sound and text. Digital signage enables a retailer to control and display their messages quickly and effectively.

Creating a digital signage system involves building a network of electronic devices that are controlled remotely from a central location. These devices present information via digital signage software to a targeted audience. Digital signage devices in the network may be plasma or LCD monitors, kiosks, projection displays, HDTVs or other electronic devices.

Using digital signs in a retail environment has many features and benefits not offered by static displays and signage. Dynamic digital signage can grab a customer's attention and influence their purchasing decision right at the point of purchase. It also eliminates the high cost of creating and distributing print ad campaigns. Digital signage is instant and offers the ability to change promotions immediately for various products or particular customers. Another advantage of digital displays over static is that retailers can earn money with their digital signage network by selling advertising space to their suppliers.

Whether it is intended to build a brand, influence customer behaviour or simply provide information, the dynamic visual experience created by digital signage should ultimately increase sales. In order to achieve that goal, retailers will need to design the appropriate system.

Digital signage software and hardware can be quite expensive and therefore would require serious planning to justify the retailer's return on investment. Other considerations include deciding where the electronic devices will be located and what sign software package to use. Retailers also have choices in network connectivity and should understand the different distribution options available before building a network of in-store digital signage.

TRADE SHOW EXHIBITIONS ATTENDANCE TIPS

Reasons to Attend

No matter how small your retail business may be, the benefits of attending a trade show sponsored by vendors or industry associations far outweigh any reason not to attend. These conferences have been developed in order to give retail owners, buyers and managers the opportunity to meet existing suppliers, conduct business meetings, network with others in retail and investigate new products.

If you're currently struggling to operate your business with few to no employees, chances are you may feel like you don't have the time to attend a trade show. Consider hiring temporary help, asking family to assist or simply plan to close shop for a day in order to attend the trade show.

Once you've decided to attend the trade show, you'll need to plan ahead. To get the most from attending a trade show, you should have a strategy. Knowing what you would like to accomplish before, during, and after the show will help maximise your time. Here are some trade show planning tips:

Pre-Show Planning

— Avoid the confusion at the show by pre-registering.

- Have a goal of what you want to accomplish, such as which vendors to visit, what items you need to purchase, what seminars to attend and which new product lines you'd like to see.
- Know your inventory needs before the show. More efficient purchasing will save you money by grouping your orders to take advantage of discounts and special offers, as well as keeping you within budget.
- Set appointments with any vendor you'd like to meet with during the show.
- Plan to bring any employees who would greatly benefit from attending the trade show.

Where to Stay

- Check to see if the trade show organisers have reserved rooms at a discount.
- Make reservations for transportation and lodging early.
- Try to book a hotel very close to the trade show.

What to Wear

- Pack comfortable shoes, wear business casual clothing, and remember you are a representative for your business.
- Allow enough room in your suitcase(s) for bringing back more than you take. This includes literature, freebies, and product samples.
- Some exhibitors provide bags, but come prepared by bringing a comfortable carryall for all that literature.

At the Trade Show

- An updated show guide will probably be provided

when you arrive. Take some time to revise your plan if necessary.

— Make sure your badge is in plain sight while browsing trade show booths.
— If possible, request literature and samples be mailed instead of having to carry them with you.
— Have a pen and notebook ready for notes and use business cards to jot down information on the back.
— Take advantage of show specials, discounts and sales where they are truly bargains and needed in your store. Check freight costs and delivery dates.
— Keep track of orders placed so you'll stay within your budget.
— If you are planning to purchase any custom merchandise, bring your artwork and other files on a flash drive. Most vendors are equipped with laptops and can quickly send the data to the appropriate department.
— Take a break after a few hours to refresh, have a snack and get some fresh air.
— Leave the show a little early to avoid long lines for buses and cabs.

Networking

— Bring plenty of your own business cards.
— Don't be afraid to introduce yourself to others.
— Attend seminars and workshops if available. These educational presentations are why you came.
— Don't linger too long at each booth and don't stay in a conversation with a company in which you're not interested in doing business.

BIBLIOGRAPHY

Ailawadi, K. and Keller, K.L., "Understanding retail branding: conceptual insights and research priorities," *Journal of Retailing,* 2004.

Akehurst, G. and Alexander, N., *The Internationalisation of Retailing,* Frank Cass, 1996.

Alexander, N., "Retailers and international markets: motives for expansion," *International Marketing Review,* 1990.

Alexander, N., "UK retail expansion in North America and Europe: a strategic dilemma," *Journal of Retailing and Consumer Services,* 1995.

Burt, S., Mellahi, K., Jackson, T.P. and Sparks, L., "Retail internationalisation and retail failure: issues from the case of Marks and Spencer," *International Review of Retail, Distribution and Consumer Research,* 2002.

Doherty, A.M., "Explaining international retailer's market entry mode; internationalisation theory, agency theory, and the importance of asymmetry information," *International Review of Retail, Distribution and Consumer Research,* October, 1999.

Doyle, P., "Branding," in Baker, M.J. (Ed.), *The Marketing Book,* 2nd ed., Butterworth-Heinemann, Oxford, 1991.

Dunne, P.M. Lusch, P.F. and Griffith, D.A, *Retailing,* Harcourt College Publishers, Foxworth, TX, 2002.

Hamill, J. and Crosbie, J., "British retail acquisition in the US," *International Journal of Retail and Distribution Management,* 1990.

Harris, F. and de Chernatony, L., "Corporate branding and corporate brand performance", *European Journal of Marketing,* 2001.

Helferich, E., Hinfelaar, M. and Kasper, H., "Towards a clear terminology on international retailing," *International Review of Retail, Distribution and Consumer Research*, 1997.

Hollander, S.C., *Multinational retailing*, Michigan State University, East Lansing, 1970.

Kucuk, S. Umit, "Reducing the Out-of-Stock Costs in a Developing Retailing Sector", *Journal of International Consumer Marketing*, 2004.

Laulajainen, R., "Two retailers go global: the geographical dimension," *International Review of Retail, Distribution and Consumer Research*, 1991.

McGoldrick, P., "Spatial and temporal shifts in international retail image," *Journal of Business Research*, 1998.

McGoldrick, P.J. and Davies, G., *International Retailing: Trends and Strategies*, London, Pitman Publishing, 1995.

Pelligrini, L., "Alternatives for growth and internationalization in retailing," *International Review of Retail, Distribution and Consumer Research*, 1994.

Quinn, B., "Towards a framework for the study of franchising as an operating mode for international retail companies," *International Review of Retail, Distribution and Consumer Research*, 1998.

Ring, J., Charles W. King, and Douglas J. Tigert, "Market Structure analysis and retail positioning," in *Competitive Structure in Retail Markets: The Department Store Perspective*, Elizabeth C. Hershman and Ronald Stampfl eds., Chicago, American Marketing Association, 1980.

Salmon, W.J. and Tordjman, A., "The internationalisation of retailing," *International Journal of Retailing*, 1989.

Sternquist, B., *International Retailing*, Fairchild Books, 1998.

Tan, Thomas Tsu Wee, *Retail Management: 11 Immutable Laws*, Singapore: Pearson-Prentice Hall, 2006.